The Gods of Egypt

The Gods of Egypt

First English-Language Edition, Enhanced and Expanded

Claude Traunecker

translated from the French by David Lorton

Cornell University Press

Ithaca and London

French edition, *Les Dieux de L'Egypte* by Claude Traunecker, copyright © 1992 by Presses Universitaires de France
Copyright © 2001 by Cornell University

All rights reserved. Except for brief quotations in a review, this book, or parts thereof, must not be reproduced in any form without permission in writing from the publisher. For information, address Cornell University Press, Sage House, 512 East State Street, Ithaca, New York 14850.

First published 2001 by Cornell University Press

Printed in the United States of America

Library of Congress Cataloging-in-Publication Data
Traunecker, Claude.
 [Dieux de l'Egypte. English]
 The gods of Egypt / Claude Traunecker ; translated from the French by David Lorton.
  p. cm.
 Includes bibliographical references and index.
 ISBN 0-8014-3834-9 (cloth : alk. paper)
  1. Gods, Egyptian. 2. Mythology, Egyptian. 3. Egypt—Religion.
I. Title.
 BL2450.G6 T7313 2001
 299'.31—dc21
                                                              2001001671

Cornell University Press strives to use environmentally responsible suppliers and materials to the fullest extent possible in the publishing of its books. Such materials include vegetable-based, low-VOC inks and acid-free papers that are recycled, totally chlorine-free, or partly composed of nonwood fibers. Books that bear the logo of the FSC (Forest Stewardship Council) use paper taken from forests that have been inspected and certified as meeting the highest standards for environmental and social responsibility. For further information, visit our website at www.cornellpress.cornell.edu.

Cloth printing   10 9 8 7 6 5 4 3 2 1

Contents

Translator's Note	vii
Introduction	ix
1. The Sources and the State of Our Knowledge	1
The Sources	
History of Scholarship	
Basic Concepts	
2. The World of the Ancient Egyptians	14
Geographic and Social Reality	
Humankind	
3. The Gods and Their Universe	25
The Appearance of the Gods	
The Nature of the Divine	
Divine Space and Time	
Divine Language and Subsistence	
4. The Appearance of the Gods	42
Forms and Transformations	
Divine Bodies	
Attitudes and Attributes	

5. Divine Society — 57
   - The Family Model
   - Divine Groups
   - Hierarchy and Recruitment of Deities
6. Divine Functions — 70
   - Agents of Creation
   - Cosmogonic Procedures
   - The Organization of the Universe
   - Special Functions
7. The Gods and the Human Realm — 92
   - Means of Communication
   - Divine Presence on Earth
   - The Divine and the King
   - Deities and Individuals
8. Geography and the Gods — 99
   - Cities and Gods
   - Deities and Provinces
   - Deities of the Marches and Frontiers
   - Deities from Other Places
   - Egyptian Deities Outside Egypt

Conclusion — 111
Notes — 113
Bibliography — 127
Index — 129

Translator's Note

In this book, the following conventions have been followed in the citations from ancient texts:

Parentheses ( ) enclose words or brief explanations that have been added for clarity.
Square brackets [ ] enclose words that have been restored in a lacuna.
An ellipsis . . . indicates that a word or words in the original text have been omitted in the citation.
An ellipsis in square brackets [. . .] indicates the presence of a lacuna for which no restoration has been attempted.

There is no single set of conventions for the English rendering of ancient Egyptian and modern Arabic personal and place names. Most of the names mentioned in this book occur in a standard reference work, John Baines and Jaromír Málek, *Cultural Atlas of Ancient Egypt* (New York, 1980), and the renderings here follow those in that volume. Of the two exceptions here, one is the omission of the typographical sign for *ayin*; this consonant does not exist in English, and it was felt that its inclusion would serve only as a distraction to the reader. The other is the divine name Amun-Re, which is more consistent with the form Amun than is the Amon-Re of the *Atlas*.

This book fills a long-standing need for a concise introduction to Egyptian religion from the sure hand of a master of the subject. I wish to express my gratitude to Cornell University Press for asking me to serve as its translator, along with my thanks to the author and to Mrs. Marinette Rosenfeld for their help during the course of this project.

D.L.

Introduction

Texts on papyri, stelae, temple walls, and statues make constant reference to the deities of Egypt, furnishing huge amounts of information about them. But what disorder there is in this abundance! Accustomed as we are to the unity of the individual, even a divine one, we today find ourselves at a loss in the face of this capricious throng of sublime beings whose ancestry varies according to the sources. A geographic approach, though convenient from the point of view of an encyclopedia, is equally bewildering: local deities, however unimportant, all boast the glorious epithet "great god." As for the appearance of these beings, one of whose qualities was specifically the ability to transform themselves, this approach is more deceptive still. Rare are deities who make do with having a single function, and many are those who declare themselves to have been the Sole One at the first moment of creation. Moreover, these deities did not remain unchanged through three millennia of history. Under such circumstances, it is difficult to arrange them into groups of great and small, major and minor, cosmic and local. From one document to the next, the deities of Egypt defy such categories as they slip through the meshes of our net. Polymorphic and polyvalent, they seem to elude our grasp. Still, they exist, and they must therefore measure up to some standard of coherence.

This coherence resides in the individual document—the only ancient reality that remains accessible to us. In this religion without dogma or canonical book, the existence of the deities is divided, fragmented into as many living parcels as there are documents. Fixed in time and the work of a single person or community, these documents draw as needed and for a specific purpose on the divine world of a given place and time. Action was necessary: deities had need of humans, and the security of the latter depended entirely on the good will of the former. This action was ritual, which consisted of words and deeds that were effective, yet evanescent. In pursuit of this effectiveness, local theologians would manipulate deities and myths by combining the names, functions, and appearances of imaginary beings, blending the ancestral traditions of their town with the latest findings of their fellow ritualists in the next town, and glossing an old papyrus discovered in the temple library in the light of contemporary ideas and the goal to be attained.

In the previous edition of this volume, the late François Daumas succeeded in presenting the entirety of the world of the Egyptian deities by adopting a geographical approach. On a more modest level, my aim is to furnish the reader with some conceptual aids drawn from the "toolbox" of the ancient theologian to facilitate access to the imaginary realm of the ancient Egyptians. To assist the reader, the facts, examples, and rules are arranged according to a scheme that could give the impression of a homogenous and timeless divine society. This is a dangerous illusion, yet it is a price worth paying to penetrate this confusing world and orient ourselves in the labyrinth of the divine realm of ancient Egypt.

CLAUDE TRAUNECKER

I

The Sources and the State of Our Knowledge

THE SOURCES

Diversity of Sources

The sources concerning the deities of Egypt are innumerable. State, Pharaoh, and society were part of a universe in which deities were ever present, even in the most mundane aspects of life.

These sources can be divided into two categories: *profane* and *religious*. The former includes objects, monuments, and documents whose primary aim was not cultic but where deities were present, such as a business letter beginning with a list of deities whose protection is invoked on behalf of the honored recipient or the decoration of a mirror whose handle, adorned with the face of Hathor, employs this image of the sky goddess united with the sun to evoke the radiant allure of a young woman.

Literary texts occupy a special place among the profane sources. Texts qualified as "tales" draw inspiration from the divine world. Often, these tales are allegories with humorous allusions to political, cultural, and especially religious developments. Wisdom texts, a very ancient genre, depict a venerable personage in his twilight years imparting a collection of practical precepts to his son. These teachings paint a picture of an ideal society whose principles are based on the relationship between the human and the divine.

The most specifically religious sources include objects and monuments directly related to an official cult, a private cult, or any activity directed at the divine realm of the Egyptians.

Temple decoration is by far the most abundant source for those who wish to explore the world of the Egyptian deities. The innumerable offering scenes from the later temples depict the king, the quintessential exponent of Egyptian society, officiating before gods and goddesses who are represented and described. But these sources are also the trickiest to use, for these scenes and representations belong to series composed according to general rules of form and content that had the power to determine the epithets, functions, or even the nature, of a deity.

Major Text Corpora

Certain religious texts were handed down through the entirety of Egyptian history, added to or subtracted from, modified or glossed, reinterpreted, or illustrated. The oldest corpus (i.e., text collection) is known as the Pyramid Texts (Figure 1).[1] These texts decorate the walls of the funerary chambers of kings and queens from the end of Dynasty 5 through Dynasty 6; they comprise a group of 759 chapters that differ greatly in their length.

Some Egyptologists have seen the Pyramid Texts as a collection of disparate documents, whereas others have considered them to be texts that were recited during the royal burial; still others have viewed the texts as a sort of guide for the deceased king, along with his mythical biography. It has long been agreed that these texts have their roots in the religion of prehistoric Egypt, but that, in various ways, they refer to the structured state of the monarchs of the Old Kingdom.

Later, some of these texts, which were originally intended only for the welfare of the king, were diverted to the benefit of private persons. In the Coffin Texts, painted on the interiors of coffins of dignitaries of the Middle Kingdom, we find numerous borrowings from the Pyramid Texts. This corpus comprises 1,185 chapters; from the New Kingdom on, many of these chapters were reused in the Book of Going Forth by Day, made up of 192 chapters and better known as the Book of the Dead.

As deemed necessary, formulas from these collections could change context, passing from the funerary cult to that of the temples. The deco-

The Sources and the State of Our Knowledge 3

Figure 1. Hieroglyphs from the Pyramid Texts of the pyramid of Teti. Photograph © Al Berens, Suredesign Graphics.

ration of the Ptolemaic temples makes use of ancient chapters from the Pyramid Texts and the Book of the Dead (e.g., Chapter 17 of the Book of the Dead at Siwa Oasis).

Among the major text corpora, we must count the books known by the evocative names of That Which Is in the Duat (i.e., the netherworld), also called the Amduat, the Book of Caverns, and the Book of Gates. These important compositions originally decorated the walls of the royal tombs of the New Kingdom, but they were soon turned to the benefit of private persons, in particular the Amduat.

In the fourth century B.C.E., new funerary compositions made their appearance at Thebes. These were the two Books of Breathing, whose contents are quite disparate and present numerous variants.

Rituals

Certain widely used rituals are known to us in several versions from various contexts. The very ancient Opening of the Mouth Ritual served to quicken statues of deities and deceased persons, as well as mummies.[2] The Daily Cult Ritual, a series of sixty-six cultic acts according to a papyrus now in the Berlin Museum, was celebrated in all the temples. Its concern was the personal care of the god or goddess: the cult statue was anointed, dressed, and provided with food.[3]

Other rituals, celebrated at less frequent intervals, have also survived on papyrus: the ritual for the deified king Amenophis I, the Embalming Ritual, the ritual for the Confirmation of Royal Power, and so forth. The "divine father" Nesmin entered the hereafter provided with several rituals preserved on Papyrus Bremner-Rhind,[4] including the Lamentations of Isis and Nephthys, the Book of Overthrowing Apopis, and a litany of the names of Apopis. Nesmin's colleague Pasherienmin complemented his Book of the Dead with rituals preserved on Papyrus Louvre N 3129[5]: Protection of the Barque, Hunting Seth and His Confederates, Hunting the Evil One, the Glorifications of Osiris, and the Bringing Forth of Sokar.

Other books and rituals are known from the decoration of temples, such as the Funerary Ritual of Sokar in the Month of Khoiak and the Protection of the Divine and Royal Bed. Certain ceremonies have been described as sacred dramas involving divine personages: the Myth of Horus in the temple of Edfu[6] and the Divine Birth Ritual celebrated in the mammisis (i.e., birth houses) of later temples; we know the latter already from New Kingdom versions depicting the births of Hatshepsut and Amenophis III.[7]

Hymns, Myths, and Magical Texts

Among the best-known hymns, we must cite the two lengthy compositions dedicated to Amun now in the museums in Leiden (Papyrus Leiden I 350)[8] and Cairo (Papyrus Boulaq 17),[9] as well as the great Hymn to the Nile.[10] We must also note the famous hymns to the Aten from the tombs at el-Amarna.[11]

Some hymns—such as the Exhortations to Fear the Divine and, perhaps, the songs in the Ritual of Mut—were chanted by the crowd gathered at the gateway of a temple. There are frequent allusions to myth in stories; for instance, the Tale of the Two Brothers is based on the combat between Anubis and Bata, gods of the eighteenth nome of Upper Egypt.[12] There is also the Legend of the God of the Sea and the best-known and most irreverent of them all, the Contendings of Horus and Seth.[13] Certain cosmogonies, written to supply a mythic justification for the location of a temple, were carved along the bottom of its gateway or on its naos.

Other stories were integrated into funerary compositions; an example is the Book of the Heavenly Cow, which we know from such sources as the tomb of Sethos I and one of the golden shrines of Tutankhamun.[14] Magical texts constitute our richest source of mythological allusions.

This abundance provides us with a richness of detail, but it is also a source of difficulties, thanks to the disparate nature of the contexts of these documents and the uses to which they were put. Were these surviving witnesses to Egyptian religious thought based on some common source?

Because Egyptian religion was not founded on divine revelation or prophetic tradition, there was no codified doctrine, no canonical text in the strict sense of the term. There must have been certain basic formulas; Jan Assmann has reconstituted a series of seven standard hymns to the sun.[15] It was only from the New Kingdom on that there was a tendency to carve in stone copies of books and rituals previously recorded on papyrus; the intended goal, however, was still the effectiveness of the document at the local level.

Temple libraries, the Houses of Life, were consulted for answers to specific immediate needs.[16] Their scribes were not the guardians of a truth fixed in the texts, but, rather, learned persons who knew how to use the ancient books to assure the effectiveness of the traditional rituals and their more recent versions.

Knowledge of the divine realm was also a source of power: whereas certain text corpora, such as the Book of the Dead, were widely accessible, others were considered dangerous. Some rituals begin with terrible threats directed against the reader who might reveal their content to profane persons; according to the author of Papyrus Salt 825, anyone so indiscreet as to reveal the Osirian ritual entitled End of the Work would be massacred. Therefore, knowledge of certain deities and myths was restricted to authorized conjurors.

Lists of Deities

The Egyptians did not feel a need to make an inventory of all their gods and goddesses. The efforts of the Hittites, who drew up lengthy concordances between their deities and those of their neighbors, would have made the Egyptians smile. The lack of such inventories was due to the very nature of the pantheon, in which deities would make an appearance, disappear, or change their names or functions according to circumstances. Such lists known to us were made within a limited context and for a specific purpose. The tomb of Ramesses VI is a monument dedicated to all the gods of the Duat, for whom the king "drew up a new inventory to renew their names." "Telephone books" of this sort had their counterparts in the cultic *Who's Who* of the manuals of religious geography, such as in the Book of the Faiyum,[17] the Geographical Papyrus of Brooklyn,[18] and Papyrus Jumilhac.[19] The aim of these documents was to set forth the theological factors that consolidated the local deities in their universal, and thus ritually effective, functions (see pp. 13 and 95).

In the temple of Sethos I at Abydos, two lists contain a total of 113 deities grouped by sanctuaries and chapels. In this case, as with most of the known lists, the deities are evoked within the framework of a litany, and their number, order, and nature can vary. In the later periods, the walls of a naos (i.e., shrine), a sort of stone cupboard containing the image inhabited by a deity, often bore representations that constituted an inventory of the local cult statues associated with the deities who resided in the temple.

Such lists resemble the inventories of divine statues carved on the walls of the crypts of the temples of Tod and Dendara. The great list of deities displayed on the walls of the sanctuary of Amun at Hibis (Figure 2) in el-Kharga Oasis[20] is an inventory of the divine images honored in the major cult centers, grouped by nome, and not a tableau of the entire Egyptian pantheon.

Figure 2. Depiction of cult statues on a wall of the sanctuary of the Temple of Hibis. After N. de G. Davies, *The Temple of Hibis in el Khargeh Oasis*, vol. 3 (New York, 1953), pl. II.

HISTORY OF SCHOLARSHIP

Before Champollion

The prestige of Egyptian civilization seemed incompatible with the barbarous appearance of its deities, and this led many ancient writers, Christian and otherwise, to the notion of a religion of initiates, as opposed to that of an ignorant and superstitious people. This was the position of numerous exegetes, historians, and scholars, and it has been perpetuated down into our own time.

Egypt's strange pantheon, with its half-human, half-animal deities and other hybrid beings, inspired the Greeks to mockery and disgust. "You worship an ox, I sacrifice it to the gods" is the ironic address to an Egyptian by a character in a play by Anaxandrides in the fourth century B.C.E.

Nevertheless, the wisdom of the ancient civilization of Egypt enjoyed great prestige among Greek thinkers. According to tradition, the mathematicians Thales, Pythagoras, and Eudoxus of Cnidus, the legislators

Solon and Lycurgus, and especially the philosopher Plato sojourned in Egypt and received part of their knowledge from the Egyptian priests. "I memorized the books of Horus and Isis," says Pythagoras in a work by Lucian of Samosata. Diodorus Siculus goes so far as to imagine that Homer once made a stay in Egypt.[21]

According to Diodorus, the Egyptian priests taught a secret doctrine. Clement of Alexandria affirms that behind "the monster sprawling on a purple rug," the Egyptians "communicated truth only through enigmas, allegories, metaphors, and other kinds of figures."[22] According to the Christian apologist Arnobius (died *c.* 327), the crowd saw only the animal, whereas the sage honored the eternal concepts it embodied. In Lucian of Samosata's *Dialogues of the Gods*, Zeus himself declares, "Their religion is filled with emblems . . . and should not be mocked by anyone who is uninitiated."[23] In the third century B.C.E., the Stoic Euhemerus of Messina developed a thesis that the gods were superior humans who had been deified because of their benevolent acts on behalf of their contemporaries. In the early years of the second century of our own era, Plutarch analyzed the myth of Osiris, which he considered to be a series of allegories, to extract a transcendent vision that could respond to the questions of his own time.

Some decades after Clement, the Church Fathers scarcely bothered with the deities of Egypt, whom they relegated to the rank of demons or fallen angels at a time when Egyptian religion was still a living reality: the latest known hieroglyphic inscription that can be dated with certainty commemorates the burial of a Buchis bull in 340 C.E. At Philae, the cult of Isis was maintained for political reasons until 535 C.E.

In the fifteenth and sixteenth centuries, the works of the Greek geographers and historians were rediscovered, and pilgrims and travelers journeyed to Egypt. On the whole, Egypt seemed to Renaissance thinkers like a land where hidden wisdom was transmitted to initiates by means of hieroglyphic writing. The Counter Reformation gave fresh impetus to research, and Egypt became the cradle of a pre-Christian thought inhabited by the Holy Spirit. According to Athanasius Kircher (1652), Egyptian deities were obscure allegories concealing the incarnation of the Eternal Word.

In the Age of Enlightenment, the predominant vision was that of a religion of monotheistic initiates ruling over superstitious, zoolatrous masses:

the Supreme Being was known only to the elite (Voltaire, 1753). Like us, the Egyptians "worshiped only a sole, unique and invisible god," but "under names and forms that suited his various attributes."[24]

The year 1809 saw the publication of the first of the volumes of the colossal *Description de l'Égypte*,[25] the sum of the observations gathered during Napoleon Bonaparte's expedition to Egypt (1798–1800). For the authors of the *Description*, the secret of the initiates was not the knowledge of a supreme and unique transcendence, but of the mysteries of nature. The deities were "fanciful inventions, symbols" invoked to "depict natural phenomena and furnish them with some sort of sensible image."

Monotheism and Polytheism

From 1824 on, Egyptian religious texts were finally directly accessible. Their content, however, was as confusing as the divine images. For Jean-François Champollion,[26] Amun-Re was the supreme being. Throughout much of the nineteenth century, the predominant view was that of a monotheism that was more or less manifest or hidden. E. de Rougé (1860) and Sir Peter Le Page Renouf[27] held to a henotheistic thesis: each of the faithful chose a deity to be his Unique One. Heinrich Brugsch wrote of a theology of the Good that was innate in the human heart.[28] To Gaston Maspero,[29] myths were political events that had been transposed into the realm of the transcendent.

In 1879, Paul Pierret[30] published an account of an Egyptian religion whose central figure was the unique, hidden god who manifested himself in the sun. The deities who accompanied him were symbolic images, hieroglyphs of a sort describing the course of the sun, and the deplorable animal cults were only a late corruption. Toward the end of the nineteenth century, two events would influence the thinking of scholars: (1) the colonization of Africa and the discovery of totemistic societies (Frazer's comparativism), and (2) the discovery of the Pyramid Texts (1881), which revealed that the Egyptians of the Old Kingdom had been polytheists. Victor Loret[31] was the first to make use of the totemic model. He would be followed by Émile Amélineau,[32] Philippe Virey,[33] and especially Alexandre Moret (publications from 1925–1935). For Moret, the nomes (i.e., the various districts of Egypt) were ancient clans, each with its totem. The totemistic thesis met with lively opposition (Van Gennep,[34] Foucart,[35]

Meyer,[36] Wiedemann[37]), but the most structured objections came from Adolf Erman (publications from 1905–1937) and his students. This school of thought, which could be qualified as pragmatic, based Egyptian religious thought on a sentiment of fear in the face of nature. The archaic deities were maintained, but the evolution of their civilization led the Egyptians of Dynasty 18 toward a lofty concept of divinity that approached monotheism. The aftermath was nothing more than a long period of decadence. The evolution of theologies was the result of political conflicts and rivalries among clergies.

These ideas were taken up, refined, and developed by Kurt Sethe[38] and Hermann Kees.[39] Apart from some marginal and often comparativist theories (G. A. Wainwright,[40] the sky-god and rain; Elise J. Baumgartel,[41] the mother-goddess and the cow; Hermann Junker,[42] the archaic Great God), there was a general consensus around the ideas of Sethe and Kees. But a part of the French school of thought, represented by Étienne Drioton,[43] Jean Sainte Fare Garnot,[44] Jacques Vandier,[45] Christiane Desroches-Noblecourt,[46] and François Daumas,[47] remained faithful to the monotheism of the elite.

All these approaches fall into two extremes: (1) a pragmatic polytheism reflecting the political history of Egypt, and (2) a highly spiritual religious thought. The highly pragmatic Erman expressed regret that in some texts, a "grandiose vision of God" occurred side by side with "gross mythical images," such as the primordial egg or creation by divine spitting. In these reactions, we find the implicit idea that all religious thought ought to lead toward the concept of a sole transcendent deity. One writer went so far as to wonder "whether the Egyptians, in the last analysis, were not monotheists without being aware of it"!

The Modern School

In 1946, the Egyptologist and Assyriologist Henri Frankfort cast aside the dilemma of polytheism versus monotheism and refrained from making value judgments.[48] He attempted to penetrate the logic of the ancients, and he introduced the notions of deities as forces of nature, a theology that described the universe, a multiplicity of approaches, and multiple points of emergence. The syntheses proposed from the 1960s on by Philippe Derchain,[49] Serge Sauneron, and Jean Yoyotte[50] are based on these concepts. In 1971, Erik Hornung published a definitive work on the divine world of Egypt,[51] and it has enjoyed a rather large consensus. Since 1975, Jan Assmann,[52] a specialist in solar hymns, has published a series of studies in which he has relaunched the debate concerning the apparent contradiction between a largely polytheistic divine realm and the concept of a single deity (see p. 88).

BASIC CONCEPTS
Multiplicity of Approaches

The gods and goddesses were the animating forces of nature, which constitutes the category of *reality*. Despite its infinite diversity, the real is in fact a whole. An object has only a palpable and quantifiable reality. But beyond the real of human experience, there reign the ordering forces of the world, which belong to the category of *truth*. This truth contains all the potentialities of the imaginary. For modern physics, the real and the true are supposed to be superimposed. But the ancient Egyptians saw things differently: if the real was a whole and thus a unique entity, the truth was multifaceted as a consequence of the fact that it was not immediately accessible. The multiplicity of truths, and thus of mythic descriptions of the world, authorized a diversity of responses to the questions posed by humans as they observed nature. This *multiplicity of approaches* permitted the juxtaposition of apparently contradictory mythic images. Thus, it did not matter whether the truth of the sky was contained in the image of a celestial river on which the sun barque sailed, in the image of a woman's body giving birth to the sun each morning, or in the image of the star-covered belly of a cow whose legs supported the sky (Figure 3). All these approaches could be superimposed on one another because function prevailed over form.

As an awareness of the ways in which the universe functioned, Egyptian religion was a sort of physics[53] that drew not on objective and reproducible data, but, rather, on plays on images, words, and metaphors. Myths described natural phenomena, and, like the models of modern theoretical physics, they employed a formal language whose symbols were deities and whose equations were the stories about their actions. By way of an example, the myth of Osiris, the god who died and was reborn

12   *The Gods of Egypt*

Figure 3. Book of the Heavenly Cow, the cow supported by Shu and the *Heh*-gods. From the tomb of Sethos I. Photograph by H. Hauser.

thanks to the care of Isis and Nephthys, was a means of expressing all cyclical phenomena, whether of vegetation, the Nile inundation, or even life and death. The basis of myth was universal, but its expression could make use of diverse theological materials. The priests of Elephantine imagined a Satis-Isis who, assisted by an Anukis-Nephthys, assumed Osirian functions in the framework of their local theology. Such associations of divine names were a means of combining persons and functions quite distinct from syncretism.

Thought and Action

Deities were immanent and present in a reality that was only a reflection of their actions. But this world, as it was recognized and described and for which Egyptians felt responsible because they had conceived of its function, was a fragile one. Its maintenance depended on ritual.

On the theoretical level, ritual was based on two concepts: (1) *polysemy* (i.e., the plurality of meanings of images, things, and objects), and (2) the *performative* nature of image and word. Many "objects" could be *points of emergence* of one and the same force, of some "thing" stemming from the imaginary. Thus, the fertility of the land was contained in the inundation, but also in the sun, which regulated its return. Conversely, a single imaginary "thing" could embody currents animating a number of "objects" in the real. The crocodile god Sobek had charge of the realm of aquatic animals and the chthonian forces of plant growth.

The bonds uniting name and thing went beyond a simple semiotic code. Speech was *performative*: to pronounce the name of a thing was to endow it with existence. In ritual, word and image, speech and act constituted a performative language. In its form, ritual fell within the category of the real, but in its consequences, it participated in the imaginary. To assure the effectiveness of a ritual, it was therefore necessary to practice it on an object that belonged to both realms. This was the role of the cult statue, the image of a divine being, which was inhabited by the *ba* of the deity (i.e., by the part of a god or goddess that was capable of crossing the border between the real and the imaginary).

Contact with the forces of the imaginary thus transpired via the image of a defined, named, delimited, and recognized divine personage who was present in the cult statue, a portable, manufactured *point of hierophany*. But the results expected from this contact were supposed to have implications for the entirety of the universe, sometimes beyond the usual attributes of the deity in question. To resolve this paradox entailed in ritual, the Egyptians extended the name of the deity serving as the point of access to the divine realm. The crocodile god Sobek thus became Sobek-Re, who was responsible for the course of the sun.

2

The World of the Ancient Egyptians

GEOGRAPHIC AND SOCIAL REALITY

The Nilotic Environment

"All the country irrigated by the Nile was Egypt and all the people who lived below Elephantine and drank the Nile's water were Egyptians"—so the oracle of Amun once proclaimed, according to Herodotus.[1] The Two Lands, as the Egyptians called their homeland, were threadlike in the south, with its 600 miles of narrow valley, and blossomed in the north into the delta, a sort of fertile triangle whose sides were 125 miles in length. This land was a fertile gem set in a desert filled with sand and rock. To the east, the mineral-rich desert was bounded by the liquid expanse of the Red Sea. To the west, beyond the chain of oases, stretched the vast deserts of Libya and the Sahara. To the south, the Nubian desert closely hemmed the river, which was obstructed by a series of cataracts. To the north, a zone of swamps infested with dangerous animals and brigands isolated the country from the Mediterranean.

Upper Egypt's landscape was highly oriented, with its river flowing northward, while the sun rose and set each morning and evening behind the ocher horizons of the eastern and western deserts. Contrasting with the pastel yellows and reds of the desert, the fertile band along the river displayed bold colors: black in the season of sowing, radiant green when the vegetation grew, warm yellow when the grain was ripe. In its midst, the sky was reflected in the broad ribbon of the Nile, which flowed from south to north. A source of fertility, the river was also a transport link uniting the entire land. Roving administrators would travel by boat, their ships becoming a sort of floating ministry. The banks were a marshy zone rich in fish and waterfowl and the nesting place of migratory birds. Crocodiles lay in wait on the sandbanks, while hippopotami lazed in the muddy waters of the river. Farther from the banks were the lowlands, the *pehu*, the first to be covered by the inundation, and then the lands that remained above water through a large part of the year. A network of irrigation canals crisscrossed the fertile plain. Water was omnipresent, even during dry periods. Anywhere in the plain, one had only to dig a ditch some feet deep to reach the water table, a sort of subterranean Nile that saturated the ground. In the delta, the vast green and black stretches of cultivation were punctuated by impenetrable marshes and sandy mounds occupied by cities. From June to November, the inundation transformed the land into a liquid expanse, from which rose cities and dikes.

The edge of the desert marks the distinct boundary between the ordered, defined world of the fertile plain and the vast, unformed, unorganized stretches of sand and sterile rock. There, scattered clumps of sycamore trees afforded welcome shade to the peasant and his cow. Rivulets occupied the low points of this zone of the valley, which was distant from the river and thus received less silt. At nightfall, these watering holes were visited by lions, antelopes, oryxes, and other desert fauna.

The overall uniformity of this landscape, which repeated itself incessantly from Elephantine to the delta, was another trait specific to Egypt. Certain places in the valley, however, enjoyed a special geographic situation. This was the case with Elephantine at the First Cataract, where the river makes its way through barriers of granite rock. Much farther north, Koptos was the departure point of a trail leading to the Red Sea through the Wadi Hammamat, an important mining area. A trail that began at Hu gave access to the western oases. A little south of Memphis, the Faiyum, a depression irrigated by a branch of the Nile, was a geographic entity unto itself. Finally, there were frontier regions, the western marches of the delta, poorly protected by nature but opening onto relatively unpopulated areas. By way of contrast, the eastern frontier—the point of departure toward Asia and the world of the Middle East—was protected by areas of lagoons where access was relatively easy to control. In the south, Elephantine controlled riverine traffic from Nubia conveying the products of Africa and the gold mines of the Nubian desert.

It was from this environment that the Egyptians drew images and metaphors to describe the universe animated by their gods and goddesses.

Natural Settings and Deities

A lioness prowls around a crescent-shaped rivulet at the foot of an alluvial fan that slopes steeply down from a cliff in the desert. It is the goddess Sakhmet (Figure 4), she who roams the desert in her fury, the "distant" goddess who, when she is appeased, comes to quench her thirst at the lake called Asheru. One of the wishes of deceased persons was to enjoy a repast while comfortably seated in the shade of a tree and under the protection of the cow goddess Hathor, mistress of joy. In one spell from the Coffin Texts, crocodiles and lions, animals that were fearsome and feared, provision the chapel of the deceased: "the Sobek crocodiles who catch fish for her."[2] Such ambivalence was characteristic of Egyptian thought. Immersed in a natural milieu on which they were entirely dependent, Egyptians conceived of nature as an unchanging whole whose components were necessary. The herdsman crossing a rivulet of water with his cattle was in fear of crocodiles, of course, but the presence of the animal was part of the order of things. The natural, permanent association of this animal with a watery milieu rich in fish and fowl also made it a symbol of an aquatic environment where food was abundant. Like other dangerous animals, the crocodile was thus an ambivalent being. In the later periods, the crocodile at Koptos, "rapid of course," was a form of Geb, the earth god. The crocodile was also a form of destiny, for "life and death were in his hands." But despite the fear they inspired, neither the crocodile nor the serpent, nor even the scorpion, was considered a priori as a harmful incarnation. This is also the case in present-day Egypt—at least in the case of serpents, which are often as respected as they are feared. In myths, however, which constitute a vast description of the cosmos in metaphorical language, the ever-present possibility of disruption of order was expressed by the image of these animals, in particular the serpent.

The World of the Ancient Egyptians 17

Figure 4. Head of a statue of the goddess Sakhmet. Detroit Institute of Arts 31.69. Gift of Mrs. Lillian Henkel Haass and Miss Constance Haass. Photograph © 1997 The Detroit Institute of Arts.

Disorder of the Waters, the Sky, and Humankind

In fact, disruption of the equilibrium of nature and society was a great source of anxiety for the Egyptians. Illness and death are tragic events, but their consequences are purely individual. To the Egyptians, such events belonged despite all to the order of things. Illness and death were the work of ambivalent deities, and otherwise entirely respectable.

There were disturbances that were much more serious, because their occurrences affected the entire land and, therefore, the universe. Despite its fertility and abundance, Egypt was a land whose economy was fragile. Exchanges of foodstuffs that were difficult to preserve occurred on the local level through bartering or reciprocal gift giving. The institution of kingship, within which we must include the temples, maintained the means of production and administered a system for redistributing surpluses. Social cohesion under the leadership of Pharaoh was assured by an ideological consensus—the concept of Maat, which has recently been studied by Jan Assmann.[3]

If the Nile did not "come in its time," famine would ensue in the land, and all would suffer: subjects, the ruling class, and even the gods and goddesses. "As the sacred loaves are pared, a million perish among men," states the great Hymn to the Nile.[4] Conversely, too high an inundation could bring serious disorder: destroyed villages, temples invaded by water. Thus, the destructive flood of 756 B.C.E. distressed the people of Thebes: "Hapy comes as you order, is he to inundate your home?"[5]

Curiously enough, earthquakes were not viewed as catastrophes but as expressions of the earth's quivering joy in the face of divine presence. Storms were among the disorders of the world. These were relatively rare in Upper Egypt, yet regular enough. Light sprinkles occurred on an annual basis, but every five to seven years, there would be a much heavier rainfall. These rains were usually viewed as a sign of divine care for the reigning monarch, but they sometimes caused a great deal of damage. Rainfall in the desert was especially dangerous, for it turned the wadis into raging, devastating torrents that poured into the valley.

Such a catastrophe struck the Theban necropolis during the reign of Ahmose. The king came in haste to take stock of the destruction: "vaults had been damaged . . . pyramids had collapsed."[6] The king had food and clothing distributed to the victims of the disaster; Ahmose acted according to Maat.

The order of nature was a reflection of political order: "everything becomes green at the sight of me," proclaims Ramesses II on a stela at Abu Simbel. Political instability disturbed the proper functioning of nature.

According to the prophet Neferti, in the time of anarchy to come at the end of the Old Kingdom, "Desert flocks will drink at the river of Egypt, / Take their ease on the shores for lack of one to fear."[7]

HUMANKIND

In ancient Egypt, the difference between humans and deities was more quantitative than qualitative in nature. People moved in the real at the human scale, whereas the gods and goddesses, endowed with immense power, acted in the true at the universal scale. Nevertheless, both groups belonged to the same creation; both were made of the same elements that supported their existence in the sensible and imaginary realms. Knowledge of these components and their role through the human model is indispensable to an understanding of the functioning of the divine realm.

Humans in the Created World

In a story from the New Kingdom, Re is the "creator of the sky and the earth, of the breath of life, of fire, of gods, humankind, large and small cattle, of serpents and fish."[8] Other texts present the creator god making humankind prior to the deities, though this anteriority procures them no manifest privilege. The humans in the creation stories are not individuals, nor even men and women; rather, they are a category of the living. By reproducing, they participate in the *creatio continua* that is visible in the world of the real, of which they are an element. Cosmogonic texts do not credit humans with any particular power over the animal and vegetable world, other than to assure their own subsistence. Re "made for them plants and cattle, / Fowl and fish to feed them."[9] Quite the contrary, humankind is readily considered to be the "cattle of the god" in the pastoral sense of the term. Vis-à-vis divinity, animals had a status close to that of humankind. Beyond the framework imposed by Maat, the principle of the social order of which Pharaoh was sole guardian, only deities had disposal of human life. In death, Egyptians definitively crossed the boundary separating the sensible from the imaginary. They joined the realm of the deities, where, after having found a new integrity thanks to the funerary rituals, they exercised new powers and enjoyed faculties previously unknown to them.

20 The Gods of Egypt

Humans in the Real

The Body and Its Shadow Living beings possessed a body (*djet*, Figure 5.1) of their own; it was sometimes called *khet* (see Figure 5.2) or *hau* (see Figure 5.3), terms that originally meant "limbs" and "belly," respectively. When the various elements of a person fell apart at death, the inert body, which was destined to rest in the netherworld, was called *khat* (see Figure 5.4). Some texts disparagingly refer to the rigid, desiccated corpse placed in its coffin as "wood." The shadow (*shut*, see Figure 5.5),[10] a sort of mobile, silent projection of the body, was part of its physical integrity. After death, it acquired a sort of independence; its role, which is not particularly clear, seems to have been associated with sexual activity. In the later periods of Egyptian history, common people tended to associate shadows with phantoms and spirits.

The Heart By means of the heart (*ib*, see Figure 5.6), a person was capable of feeling.[11] The seat of emotion and feelings, the heart was the organ on which the divine acted. A large gamut of feelings was expressed through the image of the heart: for example, joy ("broadness of heart"), courage ("thickness of heart"), anxiety ("narrowness of heart"), and many other feelings as well; there was also "he who swallows his heart," which described a person who was discreet before inferiors or cautious before superior authorities. Before the divine tribunal, the deceased implored their hearts, the seats of memory, "Do not rise up against me as witness."[12]

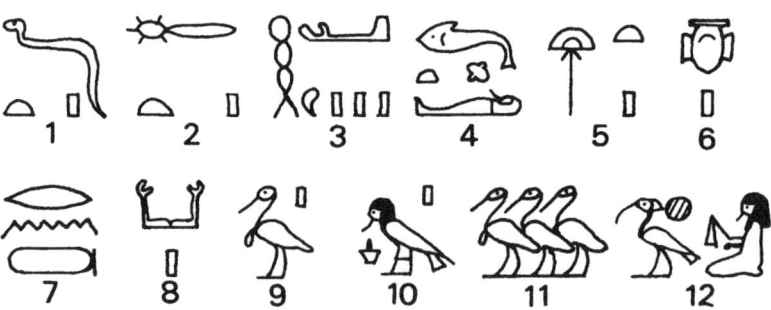

Figure 5. Hieroglyphs depicting terms for humans in the real. **1:** *djet*-body; **2:** *khet*-body; **3:** *hau*-body; **4:** *khat*-corpse; **5:** *shut*-shadow; **6:** *ib*-heart; **7:** *ren*-name; **8:** *ka*-spirit; **9:** *ba*-bird; **10:** *ba*-bird; **11:** *ba*-birds; **12:** *akh*-spirit.

The heart was also the seat of the mind, of the faculty of conception (*sia*). The "words of the heart" were thoughts, and a person without a heart was, above all, an imbecile. Lack of thought and loss of consciousness menaced one whose heart distanced itself. The seat of decisions, the heart was also that of free choice and thus of temptations. "Do not fling yourself into the arms of your heart," a teacher admonished a pupil whom he suspected of displaying more taste for the tavern than for the schoolroom.

The Name Without a name, a person was assuredly nothing. By receiving a name (*ren*, see Figure 5.7), a person became an individual, differentiated, locatable, and part of a group through his or her ties while at the same time possessing a personality, a recognized identity, and a destiny. The effectiveness of a ritual could be assured only if its beneficiary was named. Humans and deities depended on rituals, and knowledge of the names of beings was the essential condition of acting on the world. Petosiris implored visitors to his tomb, "Pronounce my name with a sincere heart, read the inscriptions, perform the rituals on behalf of my name."[13]

The potential power of the name was also a source of vulnerability. Magicians and other sometimes ill-intentioned ritualists were not unaware of the power attached to knowledge of a name. By modifying a name or by using it in rituals for ends that were sometimes scurrilous, it was easy to make an attempt on the designated person or even to derail a being in the imaginary realm. Finally, to efface a person's name from his monuments was tantamount not only to effacing his memory in this world but also to depriving him of subsistence in the next one.

Humans in the Imaginary

The Ka In the scenes of the royal birth from the temple of Luxor, the newborn child is followed by a second child whose head bears a symbol composed of two upraised arms and called *ka* (see Figure 5.8). For a long time, scholars translated this term, attested from the most ancient periods on, as "double." Some scholars even wished to see in the term a sort of guardian angel or spiritual body that evolved in the tomb. *Ka* was a vital force, understood not in the sense of a global, theoretical power, but as *the* life of everyone at the scale of the differentiated individual.[14] The king "presided over all the living *ka*s." The notion of *ka* rested on a simple physiological observation. The maintenance of every living being entailed the need to take nourishment. In nourishment, there was thus an element, a force that maintained life and enabled growth, a power that accompanied an individual throughout life. In the Middle Kingdom, there appeared a term *kau* meaning "food." If one ceased to eat, life came to an end. Nestled in an individual, *ka* was the creative force that constructed and maintained his or her body. "You are my *ka* that is in my body, o Fashioner (Khnum) who makes my body healthy."[15] It is thus natural that the *ka* was connected with well-being: "for your *ka*," was the statement of serving girls presenting a cup to a guest at a banquet. By temporal extension, the *ka* could be the seat of wish or desire: "the good will (*ka*) of the king." The four earthly benefits to which persons of merit aspired—wealth, longevity, a happy old age, and progeny—were personified by four *ka*s. Conversely, a person's *ka* could suffer as a result of excesses: "the greedy one endangers his *ka*."[16] As a sort of reflection of the energy and the moral health of the individual, the *ka* was fundamentally personal and was often merged with the name (*ren*) and, in the Late Period, even with destiny, a mark of temporal differentiation.

When a person died, his or her *ka*, a sort of capital of life that had been stored up during existence on earth, crossed the frontier of the imaginary realm. Beyond this sudden dislocation of being, the individual would subsist by means of his or her *ka*. The deceased, "the one who has united with his *ka*"— or more precisely, the one whose existence has become that of his *ka*—retained the ability to maintain his vital force thanks to the life contained in the foodstuffs of the funerary offerings presented to his name.

The *ka*, the static potentiality of subsistence and life, was an early conceptual response of the Egyptians to the challenge of life and death. But as thought evolved regarding a place beyond the sensible realm, it became necessary to resolve the question of passage between these two aspects of the cosmos.

The Ba The function of passage between the sensible and imaginary realms was assured by the *ba* (see Figure 5.9), a term that has often been misleadingly translated as "soul."[17] The *ba* was essentially an element of mobility that enabled passage from one realm to the other. Thus, it was the *ba* that came at the behest of officiants celebrating the cult, whether divine or mortuary, and it was also the *ba* that would cross the threshold of the imaginary to inhabit the alternative body that was the statue. Dying, a person "went to his *ka*," but not to his *ba*, for the latter was a dynamic faculty, not a static condition.

In the Old Kingdom, only the deceased king possessed this extraordinary faculty of movement. Later, private people would also benefit from the properties of the *ba*. Beginning with Dynasty 18, the *ba* was represented in the form of a human-headed bird (see Figure 5.10), an eloquent image for expressing both its mobility and its status as an element of the personality. After death, the body remained in the Duat (netherworld), whereas the *ba* flew off to the sky. The *ba* also frequented terrestrial locales that were reserved for it (mortuary chapel) or known to it (earthly home). Thanks to the *ba*, the deceased could assume various forms (*iru*) after making transformations (*kheperu*), and if need be, take on a functional personality that was complete and endowed with memory.

The notion of *ba* falls under human ethology. Serge Sauneron demonstrated the existence of a verb *ba* meaning "to be immanent, present, efficient in a place."[18] The plural noun *bau* (see Figure 5.11) designates anger. This collective form seems to render the indeterminateness of a raw, mobile form of energy, as opposed to the singular *ba*, a form of energy that was mobile but peculiar to a given individual. In terms of ethology, these *bau*, which are preliminary to a violent act, are signs of a disposition to attack. They act across space, affecting a sort of transfer of energy: a wrathful look and an aggressive facial expression provoke a strong emotion in the one at whom they are directed. The enemies of Tuthmosis I were "blinded by the *bau* of his majesty."

Writings were also formidable *bau*. Whether a ritual or a magical spell, a text constituted words whose effectiveness crossed the boundary between the two realms. This ability was only an extension of the effect of words: when pronounced, they traveled across space and provoked an emotion or a material reaction in their hearer. The *ba* concept implied a transfer of effective energy across space without physical contact.

The Akh "O gods, men, venerable *akhu*, dead ones, let us go in adoration, let us exalt his *bau*."[19] In this hymn to Sobek from the temple at Kom Ombo (Figure 6), the spirits known as *akh* (see Figure 5.12) are listed after the deities and between humankind and the dead. The spirits are known

Figure 6. Temple of Kom Ombo. Photograph © Dr. Howard Schreiber and Mrs. Arlene J. Schreiber.

as early as the Archaic Period. The root *akh* includes the notion of effectiveness, but it also means "luminous."[20] In the Pyramid Texts, the deceased king becomes a celestial *akh*-spirit. The *akh* was a being with occasional power and not a state (*ka*) or a faculty (*ba*) common to all. Erik Hornung has defined the *akh* as a perfect, transcendent form of existence.[21] But lest we err: this perfection was entirely amoral, and these luminous spirits could be formidable. It was probably an *akh* that was the cause of the trembling that shook the unfortunate lady Taditpabik. "If you do not withdraw your venom from her, I shall remove your *akhu*," threatened the magician, who did not hesitate to brandish the ultimate threat: "fire will shoot up against your tomb, fire will shoot up against your *ba*."[22] An *akh* whose tomb was not maintained or whose cult was not assured could become a dangerous, wandering spirit. If the identity of an *akh* was known, the spirit was appeased by writing to it and depositing the letter in its tomb. The Coptic word derived from ancient *akh* means "spirit, demon." Such was not the status of *akh*-spirits qualified as "perfect" (*akh-iqer*). These personages, well known at Deir el-Medina, died in an aura of sanctity and received a cult on the part of their descendants.[23]

3

The Gods and Their Universe

THE APPEARANCE OF THE GODS

Older Theories

For Victor Loret,[1] the gods were ancient ethnic emblems that had assumed the status of deities. Émile Amélineau[2] and Philippe Virey[3] thought that the Egyptian deity was originally the ancestor whose cult merged with that of the totemic animal—the image of the collectivity—prior to the emergence of the concept of a supreme deity with various manifestations. Alexandre Moret (publications from 1923–1936) found the origin of the gods of Egypt in the emblems of the nomes. The king was the son of the totemic animal, itself connected with a diffuse, impersonal, and collective force similar to the *mana* of the Polynesians. The servants of the cult created images and, later, divine names. Finally, theologians created universal deities. Whereas different political centers supported various political forces, certain theologies—especially that of Heliopolis—imposed themselves on the entire land. Kurt Sethe,[4] following Adolph Erman, rejected the totemic theory. According to Sethe, the gods, ancient animal fetishes, assumed human form and became anthropomorphic at the beginning of the historical era. Gustave Jéquier[5] went further still and developed a theory of three ages: fetishist, zoolatrous, and anthropomorphic. Hermann Kees[6] cautiously rejected such schemes and considered the Egyptian deities to be forces of nature that had been deified at the local level. Each local deity was destined to become a universal god through the work of theologians backing the political power.

What we call the modern school was wary of comparative approaches. According to Henri Frankfort,[7] the earliest divine form was human, and deities remained masters of their forms of appearance. For Siegfried Morenz,[8] the birth of the gods was possible only when the individual distinguished himself from his surroundings, becoming an entity who confronted nature. At this stage of differentiation, the diffuse forces (*mana*) became personages who acted, and their action was described by myth. Such approaches are tempting but difficult to prove.

Archaeological Evidence

The earliest attestations of Egyptian deities as such go back only to the Archaic Period, *c.* 3150 B.C.E. But indications of a belief in an imaginary realm extending beyond death begin to appear in the middle of the sixth millennium before our era. Bodies in a contracted position were placed on their side, with their heads facing south and their faces turned toward the west. Near the deceased were some vases filled with grain and food to assure subsistence (Figure 7). A little later, female figurines accompanied the dead. In the Naqada II Period (*c.* 4000–3500 B.C.E.), vases with figurative decoration accompanied the deceased. These images have been seen as representations of fortified villages, farms for raising ostriches, or temples on piles, but it now seems certain that these are boats (Figure 8). It is difficult to determine the nature of these vessels: are they funerary, or are they royal or even divine barques? On the cabins, there are emblems that scholars have connected with deities known from the pharaonic period. Of the approximately thirty known emblems, only two divine symbols are identifiable: the "lightning bolt" of the god Min and the crossed arrows of the goddess Neith. To these deities we may perhaps add Re (sun disk), Horus (falcon), and even Hathor (two cow's horns). The other emblems are either vegetal elements, minerals (mountains), animals (an elephant), human (a person with upraised arms), or signs that are difficult to interpret. In any event, we must note the rarity of animals (only three examples) among these emblems, even though later (approximately 3300 B.C.E.), dogs and gazelles were buried in a private cemetery at Heliopolis.

The Gods and Their Universe   27

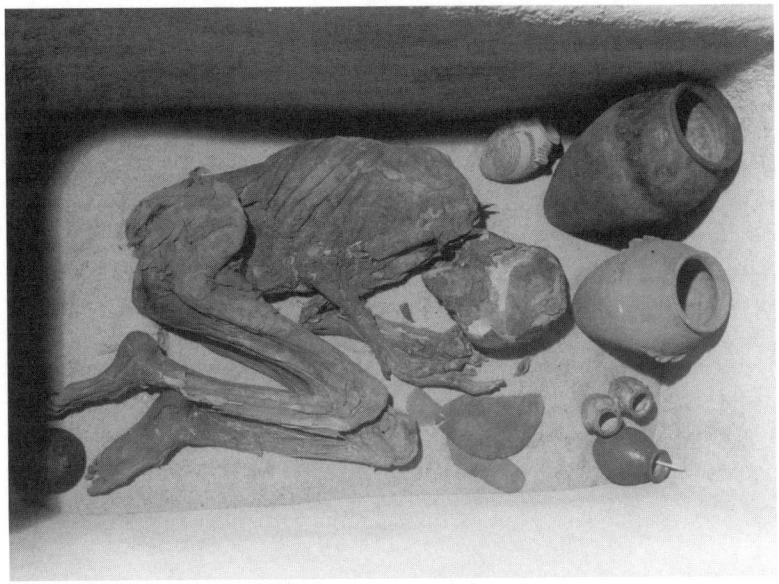

Figure 7. Reconstruction of a prehistoric burial, including a body that experienced natural desiccation. Photograph courtesy of the University of Pennsylvania Museum, Philadelphia, neg. no. S4-134562.

Contemporary Theories

It seems that Egypt of the Naqada II and III Periods was more structured than had once been thought. Traces of commerce have been found, notably in mineral products and surplus grain. Towns were essentially centers of economic organization. H. Frankfort[9] advanced the hypothesis that the chiefs of these groups were invested with religious power or, at least, magical efficacy. According to B. G. Trigger,[10] the deities and cults of these economic communities represented a criterion of identity vis-à-vis a central power. The predynastic tombs of Hierakonpolis in Upper Egypt, the city of the falcon Horus, were the sepulchers of local sovereigns whose prosperity was due to their exploitation of the gold of the eastern desert.

Scholars today think that the unification of Egypt under a single king was a process that occurred over a sort of intermediary period of a cen-

28   *The Gods of Egypt*

Figure 8. Naqada II vase with a depiction of a boat. Brooklyn Museum of Art 09.889.400. Photograph courtesy of the Brooklyn Museum of Art, Charles Edwin Wilbour Fund.

tury and a half (*c.* 3300–3150 B.C.E.), with a "Dynasty 0" between Naqada III and Dynasty 1.

The older, idealized vision of two opposed sovereigns—one king of the delta and the other master of Upper Egypt—who fought for domination of the land and whose conflict was the origin of the myth of Horus and Seth has been seriously contested. The notion of the Two Lands easily could have been one of the results of a theocratic ideology. The conflict of Horus and Seth could reflect the rivalry of the cities of Hierakonpolis and Naqada.[11] In such a hypothesis, the serpent Wadjet and the vulture Nekhbet—the tutelary goddesses of Lower and Upper Egypt, respectively—originally would have symbolized the marshes and the fertile valley (serpent) and the aridity of the desert (vulture). According to a recent thesis of John Baines,[12] the political power monopolized the manipulation of the divine; access to deities became the duty and the privilege of those in the entourage of the political power.

Thus, the origin of the deities of Egypt is lost in the mists of prehistory. The earliest iconographic documents, in particular cosmetic palettes, indicate the preeminence of animal forces (bull, falcon), but from the beginning of history on, we note a process of what Erik Hornung has called the "anthropomorphization of powers."[13] Under Dynasty 3, the deities had, as a whole, the appearance they would maintain throughout Egyptian history. Purely human forms (e.g., Ptah, and perhaps Min) were older than mixed forms combining a human body and an animal head— forms which only appeared toward the end of Dynasty 2 (Horus). But apart from these few examples, we have no way of reckoning the antiquity of the deities who appear in the written documents contemporary with the first two dynasties.

THE NATURE OF THE DIVINE

Terminology

In ancient Egyptian, the word "god" was expressed by a root with three consonants that we pronounce as *netjer*. This word was preserved in Coptic in the form *nute*; it was used to designate the single God of Jews and Christians, and pagan deities as well. A number of etymologies have been proposed to elucidate the original meaning of this group of consonants: "he of the natron," "he who rejuvenates," and so forth.

The hieroglyphic sign for *netjer* represents a flag on a pole (Figure 9.1). On an ivory tablet dated to the beginning of Dynasty 1, these poles are raised in front of the enclosure of a deity connected with archery, probably the future Neith.

All sorts of interpretations of the hieroglyphic sign for *netjer* have been proposed: flag, ax, or sacred weapon (Champollion[14]), mast with banners (Sethe[15]), fetish (Jéquier[16]). More recently, J. Baines[17] has proposed to see in it an archaic bannered mast dispossessed of its divine images with the installation of the sole monarchy and the secret cult. From Dynasty 5 on, detailed representations show that the object was bandaged. For E. Hornung,[18] the

Figure 9. Hieroglyphs depicting terms for the nature of deities. **1:** *netjer*-god; **2:** *netjer*-god; **3:** *djeser*-sacred; **4:** *sekhem*-force; **5:** *akhet*-horizon; **6:** *Duat*-netherworld; **7:** *neheh*-eternity; **8:** *djet*-eternity; **9:** *neheh* and *djet* holding the pillars of the sky.

bandages indicate an object charged with power. The original nature of this symbol was undoubtedly forgotten during the historical period.

Two other signs in the writing system that designated divine beings were the falcon (see Figure 9.2) and the seated, bearded man holding the "cross of life." The rapid flight of the falcon, its effectiveness, its agility, and especially its ability to soar for great distances high up in the sky impressed the Egyptians. The latter sign displays a human image of the divine being. Dimitri Meeks[19] has proposed a highly seductive approach, inquiring "downstream" into the usage of the root. It appears that ritual is constantly correlated with the notion of *netjer*: an entity becomes or remains *netjer* only through ritual. The adjective *netjery* ("divine") signifies "ritualized."

There were many objects, places, and beings that could be qualified as *netjery* ("divine"). However, apart from the king, living humans could not benefit from this interesting possibility. With regard to the king, this qualification applied especially to his function, not his person.

The term *djeser* (see Figure 9.3),[20] which we habitually translate as "sacred," derives from an ancient verb of motion whose semantic evolution covered the meanings "cleanse, repel, separate, isolate." A sacred place was one that was pure, singled out, isolated, materially fit to receive and shelter the image or object inhabited by a divine power. It can be said that, originally, *djeser* was the quality of a container whose content was *netjer*.

Divine Names

As a means of identifying a divine force, the divine name often was directly related to the nature of the deity. To attribute a name to a deity was to isolate, recognize, and define a force.

Programmatic Names, Epithets Certain names relate directly to manifestations of divine power: Khons, "he who goes and comes," a lunar deity; the jackal Wepwawet, "he who opens the road"; the panther goddess Mafdet, the "manhunter"; the lion goddess Pakhet, the "slasher"; Amun, the "hidden one," the ancient god of the wind, a powerful but invisible element. Other names are deified abstractions: Hu, "speech"; Sia, "thought"; Heka, "magic." Sometimes a name refers to a place: Satis, "she of the island of Sehel"; Nekhbet, "she of Nekheb"; Horus, the "distant/high one." Still other names allude to myths: Hathor, the "house of Horus"; Nephthys, the "mistress of the house"; Montu, "he who binds (enemies)." Some goddesses have names that are feminine doublets of gods' names: Amaunet (Amun), Rat (Re), Temet (Atum). Some names are programmatic epithets: Nekenher, "he with the frightening visage" or the formidable guardian, "he who sees with his rear."

But many names, especially those of the most ancient deities, have no etymology that can be recognized with certainty: Min, Geb, Anubis, Sobek, Re, Thoth, and so forth. Scholars and theologians were not hindered by this fact, and they attempted to enrich knowledge of these deities by inventing new etymologies. Isis found Horus, but she was seized by doubt: "Is it he? (*in pay-pu*)," she asked Thoth, and the scribe of Papyrus Jumilhac concluded, "Thus existed his name of Anubis (*Inpu*), and every royal child is called by this name because of that,"[21] thus justifying a tradition that made Anubis the son of Osiris and one of the names of royal sons.

The Power of the Name The divine name was the bearer of the reality it designated, and knowledge of it was an indispensable tool for the ritualist and a weapon for the magician: "I shall make this formidable god whose name I shall pronounce rise up against you."[22] The power of a name could even be turned against its owner. This was a dangerous, ambivalent game that must have tempted many a person. The king himself denied having tried to constrain the gods: "I have not pronounced the name of Ptah-tanen."[23]

The Secret Name Gods and goddesses endeavored to keep their real names secret. Knowledge of such real names enabled humans to appropriate powers reserved for deities.

A book of magic relates how the cunning Isis succeeded in forcing Re to reveal his secret name.[24] The goddess fashioned a serpent to bite the supreme god. The god suffered terribly, but instead of using her magic, Isis submitted Re to an odious blackmail: "Tell me your name, divine father, for he who is called by his name lives." Re then recited his names, drawing a tableau of creation, but the "living fire" of the venom continued to torment him, for, said Isis, "your name is not in what you have told me." In extreme agony, for "the venom became more powerful (*sekhem*) than live embers," Re capitulated: "Let my name leave my body to (go) into her body." The secret was kept by means of this physical transfer, and no indiscreet ear, not even a divine one, was able to intercept Re's power.

The secret name of Re was unpronounceable, for it was beyond linguistic reality. Its power was such that the story of how it was revealed to Isis, written on papyrus and dissolved in beer, was a sterling remedy for expelling venom from the body of someone suffering from snake bite. Magicians sometimes employed foreign-sounding divine names, strings of sounds barbarous to the Egyptian ear that perhaps contained secret names: Isteresek, Iterseg, Hergen.[25]

Another method used by deities to place themselves beyond the reach of ill-intentioned persons wishing to appropriate their names was to multiply their names. Amun was the god "with many names, unknown in number."[26]

What was the secret of the divine name if it one day had to be revealed? The name attempted to protect the divine personality in two opposite ways: by concentrating the divine essence in a place that was inaccessible, and, conversely, by diluting it in the diversity of the universe. The first way was the dream of magicians hoping to dispose, in a few concentrated syllables, of a divine power that would enable them effectively to alter the natural order of things and combat the effects of venom. The second way expresses the enormity of divine power, the extreme variety of its manifestations and thus the impossibility of describing and naming all the facets of a deity's sphere of action. Tortured by the venom of Isis's serpent, Re pours out his list of names, feverishly launching into a description of his accomplishments: "I am he who made heaven and earth. . . . I am Khepri in the morning, Re at noon, and Atum who is in the evening."[27] Theologians and ritualists were not confronted by the urgent situations that magicians were obliged to face. Quite the contrary, for them, exploring the nature of deities consisted in discovering, explaining, and multiplying their names: "I cause your hidden names to grow for you, I multiply your manifestations (*kheperu*)."²⁸

The Elements of the Divine Personality

Ba *and* Bas   We have seen that *ba* included the notion of the transfer of energy, the ability to cross a boundary from one realm to another and act. The *ba* of a deity was commensurate with the magnitude of his or her power. It manifested itself to the living according to the characteristics of the deity. It was the deity's visible face in the sensible realm of divine action.

"The wind, it is the *ba* of Shu; the rain, it is the *ba* of Heh (liquid space); the night, it is the *ba* of Kek (darkness); water, it is the *ba* of Nun (the primordial ocean); the ram of Mendes, it is the *ba* of Osiris; the crocodiles, they are the *ba* of Sobek."²⁹ These natural *ba*s-forces are known from the Old Kingdom on. The stars were the *ba*s of deities. Nut was "she of the thousand *ba*s," the goddess of the celestial vault. Orion was the *ba* of Osiris. Even when they were devastating, natural phenomena were divine *ba*s. From the Middle Kingdom on, a natural catastrophe was the manifestation of the *bau* of a wrathful deity. The storm that ravaged Thebes in the reign of Ahmose was a "manifestation (*kheperu*) of the *bau* of the god" (see p. 18).

To account for the many domains in which the important deities intervened, theologians broke the divine *ba* into various faculties. Receiving individual names, these *ba*s became entities in their own right. Thus, in the New Kingdom, Re was provided with four *ba*s, ram-headed personages named Manifest-Form, Magical-Power, Glorification-of-Flesh, and Integrity-of-Flesh. Later, undoubtedly to reconcile the number of Re's *ba*s with his fourteen *ka*s, Pure-of-Body, Male, and Ejaculator were added to obtain a total of seven *ba*s. The universality of Amun's power was expressed by ten *ba*s (see p. 88).

Ka *and* Kas   A passage from the Coffin Texts credits Re with a "million *ka*s," which he created to "protect his subjects."³⁰ As we have seen, these millions of *ka*s were all the natural elements that sustain life. The passage treats them as an unrefined and undifferentiated infinity. Conversely, the theologians of the Ramesside Period prepared an inventory of the blessings bestowed by Re in the form of fourteen *ka*s: nourishment, venerability, food production, greenness, victorious power, brightness, order (*was*), abundance of food, fidelity, magical power, flashing, vigor, luminousness, skill.

The Shadow The shadow of a deity signified two things. The first was protective: "Do you not know that the shadow of the god is upon me?" said King Piankhy of Dynasty 25 to one of his adversaries.[31] The second was specific to Re: shadow-of-Re (*shut-Re*) was the name of cult places that were open to the sky. How could a shining body have a shadow? In the shadows-of-Re, offerings were presented directly to the deity as he traversed the sky. The sunlight (*shuyt*) was here a dynamic element, a sort of means of communication between the distant god and the human realm. We know that the space separating sky and earth was essentially a space of communication incarnated by the god Shu, "he who unites." Shadow-of-Re seems to be a metaphor for sunlight as a power of communication, the visible projection emanating from the sun disk, a sort of *ba* manifested in the confrontation between humans and the divine object. In several texts, the divine shadow is related to the decoration of the front of temples, the designated spot of the divine image, where the exhortations to fear the divine were chanted.

The Divine Heart The creator god conceived his creation in his heart, the organ of the intellect. Later, it was his heart that took note of the state of the sensible realm: "Every city is placed under his shadow so that his heart can go there according to its desire."[32] In the Daily Cult Ritual, when the god awakes, he is presented with a heart, an image of his regaining consciousness after the lethargy of sleep.

The Akh Only occasionally did a deity deign to assume the form of an *akh* to take on a human nature. Because the myth of the royal birth occurred partly in the sensible realm, the divine agent assumed the appearance of a living being. Amun assumed the appearance of King Tuthmosis IV of Dynasty 18 to approach Queen Mutemwia and engender King Amenophis.

The Sekhem Deities made use of other instruments of power. Re was a "*sekhem*-force in the sky"; Amun was "the great *sekhem*-force"; and in the Pyramid Texts, the deities are *sekhem*-forces. From the New Kingdom on, the cult statue inhabited by the divine *ba* was a *sekhem* (see Figure 9.4), an image of power. The word is preserved in Coptic under the form *shishem*, with the meaning "shadow, phantom, specter." But unlike *akh*, which was a magical ability, a form of effectiveness modeled according to a need or a precise goal, the *sekhem*-force was an impersonal power par excellence—a raw, undifferentiated force that could be used by any deity, any being of the imaginary. The goddess Sakhmet was ordered by Re to destroy humanity when it rebelled.[33] She became the incarnation of a blind power that roamed the world, making herself drunk on human blood. *Sekhem*-force was raw, physical, unnuanced deed, and anyone—human or divine—could fall victim to it or benefit from it.

DIVINE SPACE AND TIME

Divine Space

Boundaries The imaginary spaces where divine beings dwelled were neither uniform nor infinite. The authority of the supreme god extended to the *djer* "limit" (i.e., to the limits of the created world, to the place where the uncreated began, the primordial ocean from which the cosmos emerged). That is where the far reaches of the celestial imaginary began: "The far region of the sky is plunged in darkness, one does not know its boundaries to the south, the north, the west, the east . . . this land is unknown to the gods and the *akhu*."[34] But the uncreated was not dismissed to an indeterminate infinite. As a sort of counterpart of the organized cosmos, it was omnipresent, "it extends beneath every place." In fact, in the depths of the cosmos, there slept the waters of precreation, Nun. The reality of the water table of the alluvial plain of the Nile was the origin of this image. Nun was a sort of enveloping, liminal space and the ultimate refuge of the creator god.

The Distancing of the Divine In primordial times, humans and gods inhabited the same space under the sovereignty of Re. The separation of the spaces of the real and the true was a consequence of the failure of that cohabitation. When humankind rebelled against the solar sovereign, Re decided to destroy them and retreat into Nun, the place from which he had emerged. But after the initial massacres, Re gave up the idea of annihilating creation, and he withdrew into the sky on the back of the cow Nut: "Distance yourself from them (i.e., humankind)."[35] Afterward, Re traversed the sky, shedding light on humanity from his distant presence. Despite the voluntary exile of the gods, who remained sulking far from humans, creation was saved, though with imperfections due to its new status.

Nearly every deity of Egypt could be called "lord/mistress of the sky," even the most chthonic of them. Of the various divine spaces, none was forbidden. Though he was ruler of the netherworld, Osiris was present in the astral realm in the form of the constellation Orion. The distancing of the deities into a remote corner of the sky when humans behaved badly was not confined to mythic time. During the political upheavals at the end of the Old Kingdom, "Re withdrew from humankind. He will rise and the hours will exist, (but) one will not know that it is midday, one will not distinguish his shadow . . . he will be in the sky like the moon."[36]

Nearby Spaces Earth and sky met at the horizon, the place where deities were near to humankind. The horizons (see Figure 9.5) were nearby liminal spaces where the king, deceased persons, and *ba*-souls beheld and participated in the cycle of the sun. The horizon was the this-worldly, yet inaccessible frontier between the sensible realm and the celestial imaginary. The eastern desert, and thus all the area accessible via the wadis that crossed it, was called "God's Land"—a sort of terrestrial transposition of the distant sky that was the refuge of the divine. It was the desert into which the mysterious and terrifying distant goddess retreated.

The eastern horizon was also the place where Re battled his eternal enemy Apopis, who, in the form of clouds or insidious mists, opposed the course of the sovereign of the sky. As the place where the sun blazed, the horizon was the "Isle of Flames." Sometimes provided with open double doors, the horizons were also points of communication with the netherworld, the Duat.

Duat (see Figure 9.6) was originally one of the names of the starry sky, but, from the Pyramid Texts on, this celestial realm extended into the subterranean world, thus becoming the lower Duat—a sort of lower sky into which the stars disappeared. The Duat had many features borrowed from the land of the living: islands, canals, roadways, and gates, as well as chapels inhabited by deities, spirits, and ambivalent beings who were both enemies and allies of the deceased. In the New Kingdom, the Duat belonged to the topological triad of sky/earth/netherworld. The term could designate the tomb and, by extension, all possible ills against which it was necessary to seek protection.

In an effort to achieve coherence and symmetry, the theologians of the New Kingdom assigned the different elements of the divine personality to the three spaces: "His *ba* is in the sky, his body (*djet*) is in the west, and his image (i.e., cult statue) is in Southern Heliopolis (i.e., Thebes)."[37] Here,

The Gods and Their Universe 37

the model is human, and Amun is a sort of sublime deceased person. As for humans, they had to die to reach these divine spaces.

In a ghost story from the New Kingdom, the spirit of Niubusemekh employs a curious topologic metaphor in recounting his death: "Being in front of men and behind the gods, I went to rest in year 14."[38] The expression implies the idea of a boundary that each of us must cross, one by one, and beyond which our status changes. In short, Niubusemekh's hour had arrived, and it was his turn to cross the boundary to join the gods in the space of the imaginary.

Divine Time

The Two Eternities The first of the eternities, *neheh* (see Figure 9.7), was the perpetual renewal of cycles, a periodic eternity whose rhythm was created by the course of the sun: "The route of *neheh*, it is the road of his father Re-Harakhty."[39] *Neheh* was a discontinuous, cyclic eternity, as opposed to the second eternity, *djet* (see Figure 9.8), which was continuous and linear. *Djet* was the permanence of the existing, whereas *neheh* was the eternity of its functioning.

In a vignette illustrating the Book of the Heavenly Cow, personifications of *neheh* and *djet* support the pillars of the sky (see Figure 9.9), for time and space were closely dependent on one another: *neheh* unfolded in the space created by the separation of sky and earth, whereas *djet* was the eternity of that space.

By definition, every creator deity stood at the origin of time: this was the case with Amun in the New Kingdom, but it was also true of Anukis, "mistress of the years." As for Osiris, "he remains after *neheh*."[40] The eternities of *neheh* and *djet* thus corresponded to Re and Osiris, respectively. But the Egyptians' pronounced taste for formal games and symmetries led them to associate the two eternities with other dualistic concepts:

Neheh	*Djet*
Re	Osiris
Rising sun	Setting sun
Morning	Evening
Beginning	End
Ba	*Djet* ("body")

The values of these correspondences are relative and must be read horizontally. This is just a formal game creating equivalences that are logical in structure but artificial in content. The first pair constitutes the controlling structure, whereas the second flows directly from the first through myth. The pairs that follow are transpositions of the daily course of the sun or, as in the last case, the components of the person in the grid of the eternities.

The Passage of Time Deities lived many times in the framework of these eternities. In the mortuary literature, deities and deceased persons behold and participate in the daily cycle of Re: "Your lifetime is every day."[41] Myth also knew longer periods. Later, we shall see how the Egyptians imagined precreation and the primeval eras (see pp. 72, 80, and 83).

The name of the Theban creator god Kematef means "he who has completed his time." In the spoken language, *at*, the word used to designate the creator's time, represented the smallest unit of time, as though creation occurred in an instant. In the vocabulary of warfare, *at* means "sudden attack, force."

In the myths that underlay rituals and actions whose consequences affected human society, the gods and goddesses live in human time. They are born, grow, mature, become old, and die. They are frail, precious children, like Harpokrates; vigorous and aggressive youths, such as Horus; vulnerable old men, like Re at the end of his cycle (Atum); or dead, like Osiris assassinated by Seth. But divine time differed from human time in its reversibility. Deities evidently shared in human moments, but their actions were eternal renewals, like those of Re, the inevitable metaphor for cyclic perpetuity.

The scale of divine time was not fixed like that of human time. The deities of the Judgment of the Dead "view a lifetime as an hour."[42] It even seems as though the theologians of the Ramesside Period imagined that Amun existed in a sort of transcendent time: "You have announced what will happen in the future, in millions of years, for eternity is before you like yesterday which has passed."[43]

The End of Time and the Gods The gods and goddesses were not spared the ineluctable, and the end of *neheh* would bring their disappearance, while the earth would be flooded by the waters "as at its beginning, and neither god nor goddess will remain."[44] The survival of Osiris and Atum, though confined in Nun, would assure a potential renewal of the cycles of *neheh*-eternity. In Egypt, this threat was permanent, but nothing would be definitively lost.

The constant fear of the Egyptians was the stopping of time, which could happen if Apopis ever succeeded in immobilizing the sun barque. The distress of Isis before her nursling in agony was such that the barque of the sun came to a halt: "darkness reigned, and light disappeared. . . . the seasons were no longer distinct, forms and shadows were confused."[45] This terrible situation would persist as long as the venom that burned in the little Horus—but also in any humans bitten by a venomous animal—remained unvanquished by the magic of Thoth.

DIVINE LANGUAGE AND SUBSISTENCE
Divine Language

In what language did the deities of Egypt express themselves? This question did not occur to the ancient Egyptians. For it to have any meaning, it would have been necessary to recognize the differentiation of languages and to introduce it into the divine sphere. In the earlier periods of history, non-Egyptian speakers, barbarous and incomprehensible, were viewed as signs of the imperfection of the outside world. The earliest evidence for reflection on the diversity of languages dates to the end of Dynasty 18: in his celebrated hymn to Aten, Akhenaten credits his god with the differentiation of languages[46]—a theme that would be repeated in universalizing hymns to the great creator gods. In classic theology, this function fell naturally to Thoth, the god of writing and knowledge: "O Thoth, who separated languages from land to land. Khnum (distinguished) the color of skin from one to another . . . he changed their tongue to (create) languages."[47] For the Egyptians, foreign languages were due to differences in the physical constitution of the organ of speech. Ramesses III had the Egyptian language taught to prisoners of war: "He changed their language so that they would tread the (right) path."[48] Egyptian, the language of the *remetj*-people, was also that of the deities who created them in their image. The expression "divine words" designated not only the hieroglyphic writing system but also the language of the ritual texts. The introduction of deceased foreigners into the netherworld implied that deities understood the languages of neighboring people. In the second section of the Book of Caverns, a deity named Interpreter appears in Re's entourage.

When Greek became the second language in Egypt, certain deities became bilingual. The prestige of the language of the political power was so great among the Egyptian peasants of certain villages in the Faiyum that they did not hesitate to have the questions they addressed to the oracles of their Egyptian deities written in Greek.

The idea of a divine, nonhuman language made its appearance during the New Kingdom. It had its origin in the observation of nature. At sunset and sunrise, the baboons became restive: "they declaim and they cry out for him," while the inhabitants of Egypt "hear the words of jubilation of the land of Utenet (i.e., the eastern horizon)."[49] Those who understood the mysterious language of the baboons comprehended the mysteries of Re. As the ideal officiant, the king was instructed in the secrets of this divine language; he "understands the secret language spoken by the *ba*-souls of the east."[50] This knowledge enabled him to officiate in the morning and evening before the altar of Re in the solar chapels. One scholar has connected the appearance of the divine language of the baboons with the introduction of the spoken language into written literature and administrative documents, with the result that the classical language was relegated to the status of a priestly and ritual language, as incomprehensible to the average Egyptian as the cries of the baboons expressing their joy before the plenitude of the sun disk.[51]

Divine Subsistence

The gods and goddesses lived on offerings: it is said of the Nile, "You are their life, (for) when you come, their offering loaves are multiplied, and their altars are abundantly supplied."[52] This material subsistence left the deities dependent on humans and the vicissitudes of reality. During the troubles that marked the end of Dynasty 19, the deities were mistreated "in the same way as the people, and offerings were no longer consecrated in the temples."[53] Food offerings alone, however, even when they conformed to the prescriptions regarding purity and dietary taboos (e.g., no pork, no fish), did not suffice to maintain the divine forces. These forces were nothing without ritual and efficacious speech. Incense (*senetjer*, "that which sanctifies") was given to the divine statues "as nourishment every day, in order to give strength to the Lord of the Diadem."[54] The economic health of the country, and thus of its temples, signified social consensus, which was a factor of equilibrium between humankind, creation, and the gods and goddesses. It was the reign of Maat. Ritual offerings, whether alimentary or otherwise in nature, were thus symbolically represented by the offering of a statuette of Maat, daughter of Re. The texts proclaiming that a deity "lives on Maat" are innumerable. Jan Assmann has demonstrated that Maat was also life-giving speech.[55] To evoke a deity or a being of the imaginary in the framework of ritual was to contribute to his or her existence and subsistence.

4

The Appearance of the Gods

FORMS AND TRANSFORMATIONS

Nothing was more changeable than the appearance of Egyptian deities. No more than their names, their graphic or plastic forms did not suffice in themselves to express their nature. On the stela that he dedicated at Abydos, Amenmes exalts the instruments of divine polymorphy: "Many are (your) names, sacred (your) *kheperu*-transformations, secret (your) *iru*-forms in the temples."[1]

The first of these terms, *kheperu*, is derived from a root that means "to exist, come into existence, transform." *Kheperu* are the products of an ability to transform that is constantly in action. For example, the sun god's changes of appearance and name during his daily course are part of his *kheperu*: he is Khepri in the morning, Re at midday, and Atum in the evening, with each stage corresponding to a phase or aspect of the heavenly body. When they passed into the divine realm, humans also aspired to a multiplicity of *kheperu* that would enable them to transform themselves into a divine falcon, lotus, deity, phoenix, and so forth.[2]

The term *iru* is derived from the verb *ir* ("to make"), and in the text cited above, it is applied in principle to the god's forms of appearance in the temple (i.e., to his cult statues "made" by human hands). Knowledge of the secret of the *iru*-forms of a deity was, in fact, the prerogative of the artisan-priests charged with manufacturing these cult images.

The primary meanings of these terms seem to oppose the *kheperu*, the cosmic and natural transformations, to the *iru*, the earthly appearances of divine personages. But it is not rare for the same appearance to be designated by one or the other of the two terms. In a hymn to the rising sun, the heavenly body is at one and the same time a "transformation (*kheper*) of the lord of transformations" and "the beautiful form (*iru*) of the god of the morning"—a rhetorical play combining the two approaches: a moment in a constant and multiple transformation (*kheper*) and a stage that is more or less stable in time, an immediate and present appearance (*iru*). Sometimes, by a reciprocal extension of meaning, *iru* and *kheperu* are used interchangeably.

Despite the multiplicity of their appearances and the universality of their competencies, the gods and goddesses retained their individuality. Erik Hornung has noted, for example, that Amun-Re, a god who was, to a large extent, universal, never had the appearance of "the moon, a tree, or a stretch of water."[3] In most cases, it is impossible to ascribe to each deity a unique, specific appearance expressing his or her nature. Thus, we must take the various elements in descriptions of divine appearance to be the words of a metalanguage.

DIVINE BODIES

Anthropomorphism

From the dawn of civilization in Egypt, religious thought was heavily influenced by anthropomorphism. The human form, and especially the face, were often signs of a royal or ancestral function. Deities had bodies, with a heart to imagine the world, and to conceive, love, and hate. They had eyes and ears, they saw and heard, and they had hands to act: Amun was "the one who remained unique, with many arms."[4] Certain deities were provided with a multitude of eyes. These multiplications of divine organs were functional images expressing the extent of a deity's powers, not a description of a monstrous being. Magicians and ordinary people sometimes employed these images as amulets. Personifications of concepts were always anthropomorphic, and their sex was consistent with the grammatical gender of the word they incarnated. Figurines of dwarfs, those unusual adults with the appearance of children, with a scarab on their head (called Ptah-Patoikos), were the human transmutations of the sun as an "old man who was rejuvenated."

Materials, Colors, Aromas

The substance of a divine body was composed of precious materials: "his bones are silver, his flesh is gold, his hair is genuine lapis-lazuli."[5] This description of Amun evokes a cult statue, but the materials possess a symbolism of their own. From the Middle Kingdom on, numerous texts affirm that gold was the flesh of divine beings, while as early as the Pyramid Texts, gold was the reflection of the splendor of the sun. Amun-Re illuminated the sky with "the gold of his face." All of these materials transposed the natural colors of human bodies into imperishable materials. But, when he traversed the netherworld, the body of the sun at night was of an eminently perishable material, *iuf* ("flesh, meat"). Thus, his rebirth at dawn was all the more glorious.

In representations, it transpires that the bodies of deities were decorated with colors related to their nature: Amun's flesh was sometimes blue, as suited a deity related to breath and wind; the flesh of Osiris was green, an image of the putrefaction of a cadaver and of the rebirth of plant life, or black, the color of the rich soil of Egypt.

Divine bodies often were described as "beautiful" (*nefer*). This beauty was metaphorical because, whereas it seems quite natural for Hathor, the sky goddess and mistress of love, what are we to think of the exaltation of the beauty of Sobek, the crocodile god? The concept of *nefer* expressed a harmony of function. Min's "beauty" was his phallus. Divine bodies had many other physical qualities as well, in particular, an exquisite aroma. It was this divine fragrance that enabled Queen Ahmes to identify Amun entering her chamber after assuming the guise of her husband, Tuthmosis I. Queen Hatshepsut was born of this encounter.

The Age of the Deities

According to his nature, the body of an anthropomorphic god could be that of an adult or that of a child. The child was always a little boy, approximately two years of age, nude, his index finger touching his lips in a gesture suited to his age. Young girls did not have access to the divine iconographic code. Instead, goddesses were always represented as nubile,

The Appearance of the Gods   45

perfectly formed women. Adult gods had the appearance of a man in his prime. In the case of warrior son-gods, like the numerous Horuses, we can imagine sturdy youths barely out of adolescence. Deities grew old and died, but the Egyptians were loath to represent these sublime beings marked by the ravages of age. The image of Atum as a stooped old man leaning on a stick was only the sign of a moment in the solar cycle.

Androgynous Beings

In the processions of deities depicted along the bases of temple walls, we often find a strange figure: a personage with a fat belly, masculine (to judge by his beard) but endowed with a heavy "female" chest, and dressed in a simple girdle that is sometimes provided with a phallus sheath. These genies, known from the Old Kingdom on, symbolize Hapy, the nourishing river. It has become a tradition to view these Nile genies as androgynous beings. Hapy was male, however, for in processions of genies, he alternates with female figures who also personify material prosperity. His impressive chest is that of an obese man. The image of an ideal, nourishing prosperity, Hapy displays symptoms of overeating. Happily, the Egyptians did not submit feminine personifications to the same iconographic treatment. A Demotic Text expounds a bisexual interpretation of the Nile genies: "the image of Hapy, half of which is a man, and half of which is a woman."[6]

The gender of creator deities, most often male and solitary and sometimes acting as couples, was unequivocal. The goddess Neith, creatrix of the world, was "a man acting like a woman, a woman acting like a man." One text reckons her femininity in mathematical terms: "2/3 of her are masculine, 1/3 of her is feminine," but representations show her as entirely female. The bisexuality has to do with function and not with the divine person.

Several major masculine deities are qualified as "father and mother": for example, Amun, Aten, Osiris, Sokar, and so forth. This bisexuality is not an androgyny of nature but a dualistic metaphor expressing the efficaciousness of the single god of origins and the extent of his action.

The vignette to Chapter 164 of the Book of the Dead depicts a woman with three heads (lion, human, and vulture) who is invoked by the name Sakhmet-Bastet-Rat. The text describing the image calls her "Mut" and specifies that she is supposed to be provided with an erect phallus. This is a case of a composite image with juxtaposing traits and belonging to the category of "pantheistic," or more precisely, "paniconic"[7] deities— hybrid beings juxtaposing several divine functions that were especially prized by magicians.

Hybrid Beings

The highly puzzling half-human, half-animal appearance of many Egyptian deities is the product of a compromise between anthropomorphic thought aiming at abstraction and the appearances of natural forces. These images are combinations of signs of identity or function and not figures in the real world.

By preference, certain deities whose principal function was difficult to represent had an entirely anthropomorphic form. For instance, this was true of Amun, the "hidden one," perhaps an ancient god of the wind, and of Atum, god of royalty.

The most frequent hybrid form associates a human body with an animal head (Figure 10). It is interesting to note that animals that arrived in Egypt at a late date (horse, chicken) and prehistoric animals (giraffe, elephant, and so forth) did not belong to this divine animal repertory. The face of a deity could be either a general or a particular mark of identity. Certain faces were specific to a single deity: the head of the ibis, for example, unequivocally reflected the god Thoth. Other forms had a range of application that was restricted to a few deities: for example, Anubis; Wepwawet, "opener of the ways"; Khentamentiu, "foremost of the west," were all canine deities. Other faces, finally, touched a wide range of deities: those with a lion's head, a mark of forces of destruction, were quite numerous. Nearly forty goddesses with a lion's head have been counted. All sky gods or aggressive gods could take the form of beings with a falcon's head. The serpent was associated with chthonic deities or the forces of plant growth.

Egyptians did not shrink from even the strangest associations. Sometimes, a sole detail of the visage suffices to evoke the animal aspect of the deity: on what are called *Hathor columns*, the charming face of the goddess is framed by cow's ears. Other forms are frankly monstrous, such as the many-headed hippopotami from the crypt of the temple of Tod that

The Appearance of the Gods 47

Figure 10. The ibis-headed Thoth and the falcon-headed Horus of Edfu ritually purifying King Amenophis II. Temple of Amada. After J.-F. Champollion, *Monuments de l'Égypte et de la Nubie*, vol. 1 (Paris, 1835), pl. XXXXV.

are supposed to represent the goddess Tjenenet, the consort of Montu. Demons and apotropaic beings made light of the sober appearance of the great gods.

Although it is less frequent, the converse assemblage of a human head on an animal's body is nevertheless well attested, as in the case of sphinxes or *ba*-birds. But these iconographic expressions rarely represent particular deities. They signify the irruption of humans—monarchs or deceased persons—into the imaginary realm and their accession to a power that was not natural to them.[8]

On the whole, the visage represented a personality, whereas the body represented a function. In each nome, the *ba*-bird of Osiris displayed the face of the local deity. Figures combining various parts of animal bodies employed the image to express associations of divine functions. Khons the Elder of Karnak, who had the body of a mummified crocodile with a falcon's head, combined the sign of the sky god with the body of the primordial being of the local theology.

Animal Forms

Certain deities had purely animal forms, such as the Apis (Figure 11), Mnevis, and Buchis bulls or the dog Wepwawet; sometimes these forms were associated with a more abstract and anthropomorphic deity such as Ptah, Re, and Montu, as in the cases of the three bulls. Many deities counted purely animal manifestations among their various forms: the rams of Khnum and Amun, the goose of Amun, the baboon and the ibis of Thoth (Figure 12), and the gazelle of Anukis. But the status of these animals varied considerably, according to whether they represented the deity's domain of action, his or her function, emblem, or even a divine incarnation that received a cult (see p. 96). In representations, anthropomorphizations of "sacred animals" made an early appearance: from Dynasty 12 on, the Apis bull could assume a human body. Sometimes, a deity's appearance did not slavishly imitate models in the natural world. Horus of Edfu—the warrior god who destroyed the enemies of Re—assaulted the rebels, swooping down on them in the form of a winged sun disk that blinded them. The *djed*-pillar, probably of Memphite origin, was considered to be a form of Osiris, the "stable one" (*djed*). From the Middle Kingdom on, it could be represented with arms holding the scepters of the god. The sistrum decorated with a goddess's head with cow's ears was a depiction of Hathor.

ATTITUDES AND ATTRIBUTES

Postures

In general, the poses of deities meant rather little. Anthropomorphic deities are represented standing or seated on a throne. Certain gods, such as Ptah, Khons, and Osiris, are represented with their bodies in profile and

The Appearance of the Gods 49

Figure 11. Bronze statuette of Apis. Detroit Institute of Arts 1994.46. Founders Society Purchase, Hill Memorial Fund and William H. Murphy Fund. Photograph © 1997 The Detroit Institute of Arts.

wrapped in a sort of sheath that gives them the appearance of a mummy. This iconography is known from as early as the Archaic Period, long before the practice of mummification, and it is not reserved for gods related to death. Some deities have a specific posture. The god Min, wrapped like Ptah and Osiris, raises his right hand, which supports a flabellum, skyward. His left hand, slipped under his wrap, holds his erect

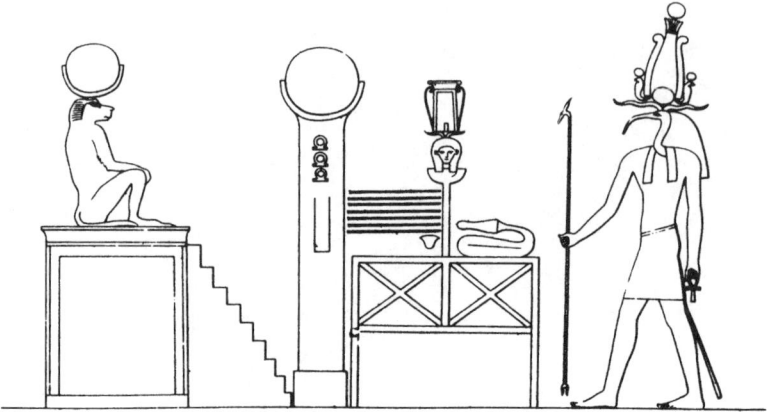

Figure 12. Thoth depicted as a baboon with a lunar disk on its head and as an ibis-headed man. Philae. After J.-F. Champollion, *Monuments de l'Égypte et de la Nubie*, vol. 1 (Paris, 1835), pl. LXXXII.

phallus. This pose was quite ancient, as evidenced by the colossal statues of Min discovered in his city of Koptos and recently reattributed to the Archaic Period.[9] Meret-goddesses, their arms raised, clap their hands to give rhythm to the acclamations of worshipers. Heh, a personification of millions of years, raises his two arms skyward. As needed, deities adopted the code of gestures common to the whole of Egyptian iconography: mourning goddesses crouch with one hand raised toward their face, whereas dead gods are recumbent, stiff in their mummiform sheath. Reborn gods are recumbent, but they raise a hand toward their face. Protectors touch the shoulder of their protégés, deities who are speaking raise their hands horizontally to lend support to their remarks, and so forth. But, in general, the poses of Egyptian gods and goddesses were sober and moderate, contrary to deities of foreign origin, who pranced about and brandished weapons (see p. 107).

Divine Accessories

The hands of deities are rarely empty. In one hand, they hold the looped *ankh*-cross, symbol of life; in the other hand, they hold the *was*-scepter (Figures 13 and 14.1–2). The latter derives, it seems, from a forked stick

The Appearance of the Gods 51

Figure 13. The falcon-headed god Horus of Edfu holding an *ankh*-cross and a *was*-scepter. After J.-F. Champollion, *Monuments de l'Égypte et de la Nubie*, vol. 2 (Paris, 1845), pl. CXXXIX (ter).

The Gods of Egypt

Figure 14. Hieroglyphs depicting terms for accessories, clothing, and headgear of the deities. **1:** *ankh*-life; **2:** *was*-scepter; **3:** *wadj* (papyrus)-scepter; **4:** *heqa*-crook; **5:** *nekhekh*-flagellum; **6:** *atef*-crown; **7:** plumed crown of Amun; **8:** crown of Ptah-Tanen; **9:** crown worn by goddesses.

designed to catch serpents. This object is known from as early as the Archaic Period, and although it remained in use in earthly life, it became the symbol of divine power. At royal coronations, deities granted life and *was*-force to the king. Like *ankh*-life, *was* was a benefit dispensed by the gods and goddesses. Because the derived verb *wasi* means "to fall into ruins," the notion *was* might be related to the forces that maintain a state. In the hands of goddesses, this scepter was replaced by a young papyrus plant (see Figure 14.3), a Hathoric symbol relating to the power of goddesses who were both gentle and terrifying.

These objects are common to all the gods and goddesses. Some deities bear insignia that are specifically related to their nature. As a royal god, Osiris, along with the mysterious Andjety of the ninth nome of Lower Egypt, is provided with the *heqa*-crook and the *nekhekh*-flagellum (see Figures 14.4–5 and 15), which were insignia of power. It is generally agreed that these two objects, which became ritual implements at an early date, were originally carried by shepherds. Certain bellicose deities, such as Neith, Waset, and Montu, are sometimes depicted as armed with bow and arrows or a mace. The intellectual Thoth holds his scribal palette.

Deities sometimes carry objects on their head, but in the majority of cases, these are signs of identification or even their names (e.g., Isis and Nephthys). Thus, Geb can be depicted as a personage with a *geb*-goose on his head. Various forms of the sun god wear a red disk encircled by a serpent, whereas lunar deities are provided with a disk and a horizontal crescent.

The divine throne assumes a very ancient royal form evoking the hieroglyphic sign for *hut* ("dwelling," see Figures 15 and 16), whereas its dec-

The Appearance of the Gods

Figure 15. Re-Horakhty with sun disk and uraeus on his head. He is seated on a typical divine throne and is wearing the regalia of a god of the netherworld, including the *heqa*-crook and the *nekhekh*-flagellum. Vignette from the funerary papyrus of the songstress of Amun Ikaiukhered, now in the Musée d'Histoire Naturelle de Colmar.

oration of multicolored bands or falcon's plumage recalls the Horian nature of the holder of power. The function of the throne is sometimes illustrated by the image of the Uniting of the Two Lands, in which two Nile genies bind together the symbolic plants of Upper and Lower Egypt; this image adjoins the lower part of the side angle of the throne. This archaic piece of furniture was allocated exclusively for the use of deities and sovereigns, while certain celebrated persons who were deified (e.g., Imhotep and Amenhotpe, son of Hapu) benefited from the comfort of luxurious chairs in the latest style during their lifetimes.

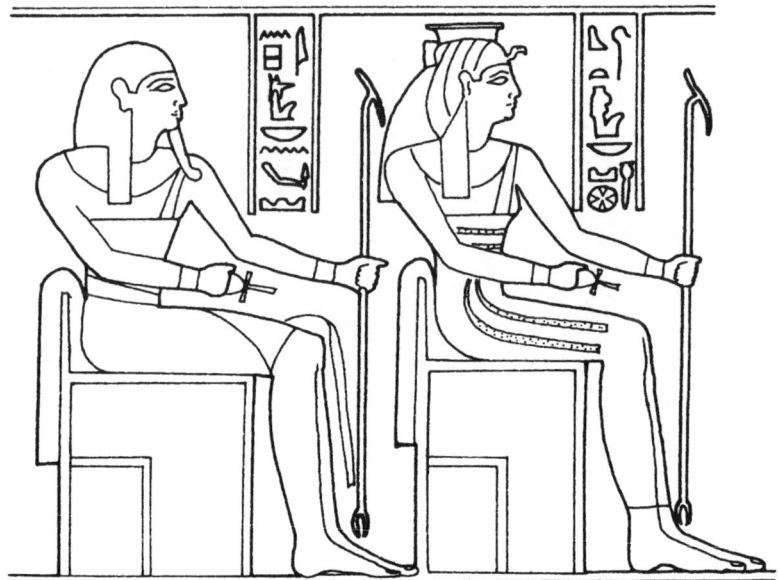

Figure 16. Anubis (*left*) and the goddess Heqat, seated on typical thrones and wearing the typical garb of a god and goddess. They hold *ankh*-crosses and *was*-scepters. From the Temple of Sethos I at Abydos.

Clothing

The principal characteristic of divine apparel is its atemporality. Males wear loincloths with a frontpiece and a sort of shirt with shoulder straps, whereas females are dressed in long, clinging, strapped dresses that begin beneath their breasts and descend to their ankles. The males also wear false beards with ends that are slightly curved. Heavy, tripartite wigs cover the tops of the shoulders—useful artifices for concealing the place where an animal head is joined to a human body. This basic costume, a sort of divine uniform, made its appearance in the Old Kingdom and would scarcely change, regardless of evolution in secular and royal clothing style. At most, from the New Kingdom on, goddesses enjoyed a sort of helmet representing a vulture whose wings enveloped the divine head.

Some details of clothing were specific to certain deities: the phallus sheath of the Nile genies, the cap of Ptah, the short-sleeved blouse of the goddess Bastet, and so forth. Deities wearing clothing of a particular historical period are deified humans. Amenhotpe, son of Hapu and of the god Ptah, wears the clothing of viziers from the end of Dynasty 18; Imhotep sports the clothes of high-ranking personages of the Old Kingdom; and Ahmes-Nofretari and Amenophis I are dressed like sovereigns of the beginning of Dynasty 18. The goddess Hathor of the West, who greets Sethos I in the netherworld, wears an ample, "flounced" hairdo that elegant ladies of his period would not have spurned, but this female wig also has an erotic connotation that accords with the functions of Hathor, mistress of love.

Crowns and Headgear

Along with the head, the headgear and the crown were elements identifying a divine image. Certain crowns were reserved for a single deity (e.g., the white crown with horns and the feathered bonnet of Satis and Anukis or the quadruple feather of Onuris), but most often, several deities wore the same headgear. Sometimes, there is a clear relationship between divine function and crown: Osiris and the *atef*-crown (see Figure 14.6), undoubtedly an ancient royal crown, or the regal god Atum and the double crown of Egyptian royalty. Divine mourning women and female servants wear modest skull caps. The head of Amun, god of breath, is adorned with two plumes (see Figure 14.7), like that of Min of Koptos. The relationship between deity and crown is often not clear: for example, what is the origin of the double feather atop horizontal horns (see Figure 14.8), the headgear worn by Ptah-Tanen and Osiris? In the later periods of Egyptian history, most goddesses wear the so-called "Hathor" crown composed of a sun disk placed between two horns (see Figure 14.9). Divine crowns combine various types of headgear. There are some late examples of composite crowns specific to a deity (e.g., the crown of Geb combining the Red Crown and the *atef*-crown), but on the whole, these crowns are in the nature of theological commentary born of the conjunction of a type of ritual act and a deity, rather than insignia identifying a god or goddess.

Images to Be Read

In sum, to represent a deity was not to reproduce the appearance of a being of the imaginary realm but to compose an image adapted to circumstances by combining various iconographic options, each with its own meaning. The result, explained by a text, is more a functional anaglyph than a fixed and immutable representation of a divine person.

5

Divine Society

THE FAMILY MODEL
Couples and Consorts
While a female deity was often associated with a male, her status was not a priori that of a wife. In Egypt, marriage had no religious basis. The predominant social bond was that which united father and son or, better, the father and his heir, the guarantor of continuity. Sometimes, the divine consort was a doublet created by the grammatical marker of the opposite gender: Sokaret, feminine version of the god Sokar; Input, companion of Anubis (Inpu); Tefen and Sesha, masculine forms of the goddesses Tefnut and Seshat. Sometimes, consorts assumed duties that complemented those of the principal deity. For example, in the Middle Kingdom, Khnum of Hur in Middle Egypt, ram-god of fecundation, was assisted by the goodly frog-goddess Heqat, the midwife: their functional association took on the appearance of a couple. Deities did not escape conjugal vicissitudes: a man from the village of Deir el-Medina discovered to his astonishment that his wife had been unfaithful and declared with outrage, "It is the abomination of Montu!"[1] Montu, a warrior god sometimes mentioned in marriage contracts, seems to have been the guarantor of happy households. On a certain day of the year, abstinence from all sexual activity was recommended, for on that day, the god Hedjhotep had behaved badly toward Montu. Was the little god of clothing a seducer?[2] A late wisdom text

attributes the existence of good wives to Mut, the divine mother of Light, and that of women of ill repute to the sensual Hathor.[3]

Procreation and Birth

The role of sexual union in procreation was known at an early era. In the Coffin Texts, Ihy, the son of Hathor and Re, recounts his conception: "It is I who was ejaculated; I flowed between her thighs [. . .] my mother made me flow (into her) while she lost consciousness of her body under the fingers of the lord of the gods, who deflowered her thus on that day of pride (?)."[4] Certain deities were born in a monstrous manner: Seth emerged from the mouth of Nut, or, according to a tradition reported by Plutarch, he violently pierced the flanks of his mother. Seth, who was responsible for the inevitable disorders of the world, was not a divine child cherished by his mother Nut. From the moment of his birth, she flew into a rage against him: "My fingers are against him like sharp knives, my fingernails are against him like metal blades!"[5]

Conversely, divine births based on the family model stressed the cohesion of the members of this family. Perhaps this phenomenon was simply a social one, because the story provided a mythological basis for the transfer of inheritance and patrilineal succession. In such a case, one had recourse to Osirian vocabulary, for Osiris was the heir of "Geb, prince of the gods," and also the disputed father of an orphan. The collective designation "children of Nut," the deities of the fourth Heliopolitan generation (see p. 75) — Osiris, Seth, Nephthys, and Horus — serves to stress family cohesion. Finally, when it came to expressing the bonds of love uniting a mother and her nursling, Egyptians had recourse to the image of Isis and her son Horus.

According to a tradition known from the Old Kingdom on, the "children of Nut" were born during the epagomenal days. These five days were inserted between the end of the year, which consisted of twelve months of thirty days each, and New Year's Day. Plutarch gives a familial version of these events. Nut, mistress of Geb, was forbidden to have children during the course of the year. But her lover Thoth, playing dice with the moon, won five days outside the year, enabling Nut to give birth.

There are some late buildings called *mammisis* that were consecrated to the commemoration of the birth myths of great gods, such as the temple of Opet at Karnak (birth of Osiris) and the temple of Isis at Dendara. Erected on podiums, these edifices are, perhaps, architectural transpositions of birthing bricks.

Child Gods

Known in some cases from the earliest dynasties, child gods were at the intersection of varied forces: power of conception, maternal love, hope of life, joy, and assurance of succession. The young Ihy, divine child of Isis/Hathor, was "the first seed of Re, well loved" by his parents. The sweet child nursed from his "mother Isis," but, as son of Hathor and heir of Re, he wore the royal crown adorned with the terrifying uraeus, and all Egypt "was in fear" before him. The little Neferhotep ("perfect of conciliation") was a child god, son of Hathor in her city of Hiw, not far from Thebes. This beautiful *hotep*-conciliation was that of Hathor: the raging goddess was transformed into a loving mother. But in the Greco-Roman temples, Neferhotep was also a procreative *ba*, a divine ram, "loved by wives at the sight of his beauty." Here, the god's "beauty" is a metaphor for his phallus, and *hotep*-appeasement is also a metaphor of Eros. Thus, Neferhotep was at the same time the child and the expression of the forces that enabled his birth.

Beginning with Dynasty 21, Harpokrates (Horus-the-small-child) assumed more and more importance, replacing or assimilating the old child Horuses. From the fourth century B.C.E. on, the birth of the newborn child, son of the local goddess, was celebrated in mammisis. These specialized buildings were the transposition into stone of birthing kiosks, light structures built in principle outside houses, where Egyptian ladies retired to give birth and care for their nurslings.

The ritual of the mammisi had its origin in the Theban royal mythology of the New Kingdom, which made the king the bodily son of Amun. In the divine version of the myth in the mammisis, the newborn baby was the local child god (e.g., Ihy and Harsomtus at Dendara and Edfu), but the divine procreator was always Amun. The ultimate goal was justification of earthly kingship—at that time in the hands of foreign sovereigns—by means of a theology of the divine child, the heir and ideal successor. From his mother's breast, the divine and royal child drank the milk of "life and order" (*ankh* and *was*), which were attributes of the gods and goddesses vis-à-vis humanity.

Families and Triads

The formation of triads was a relatively late phenomenon. It is true that the divine triad made use of the family model (e.g., Osiris–Isis–Horus), but many other associations were at work. The celebrated Theban triad composed of Amun, Mut, and Khons, for example, was quite a curious family. Amun and Mut are never represented as a couple without the child god Khons. Mut is the mother, but what of Amaunet, the feminine form of Amun, who was also considered to be his mother? As for Khons, his original nature was that of a formidable lunar deity, and although he occasionally played the role of Amun's son, his function was far removed from that of the endearing child on the model of a western family. The child god was often introduced only at a late date; this was the case with Nefertem, the offspring of Ptah and Sakhmet at Memphis. The functions of the members of these pseudo-families depended entirely on the mythic or ritual context in which they were evoked. Satis and Khnum, a very ancient divine couple of the First Cataract, adopted the goddess Anukis in the Middle Kingdom. Sometimes, Anukis was a nourishing goddess who gave her breast to the king. Although we may conclude that the family was one of the descriptive referents of divine society, this scheme was not applied to all Egyptian deities. The family model was essentially an occasional one, not a structural one.

DIVINE GROUPS

From Dyad to Ogdoad

Except for the creator god and the god of solar theologies, Egyptian deities were rarely alone. Some of them were double entities. The brutal god of the tenth nome of Upper Egypt, Antywy, whose name means "the two clawed ones," expresses in one name the violence of combat between two opposed principles—undoubtedly Horus and Seth. Ruty of Leontopolis in the delta was a leonine couple sometimes broken down into Geb and Tefnut. Any number of deities were merged into functional pairs whose symmetric interplay constituted the framework of literary or iconographic forms.

The mechanisms of association were quite varied. There was doubling: Maaty, the "double Maat" in the judgment hall of Osiris, by a contamination of symmetry with Isis and Nephthys. There were convergent actions: Isis and Nephthys tending to their brother Osiris. There were also opposed actions: Horus and Seth, the eternal rivals. We find complementary pairs: Sia and Hu, conception and expression. We also encounter geographical oppositions: Nekhbet, the vulture goddess who represented Upper Egypt, and Wadjit, the serpent goddess of Lower Egypt.

The male triad Amun-Re-Ptah of the Ramesside Period was the product of a globalizing theology that associated the gods of Thebes, Heliopolis, and Memphis, the great intellectual centers of that era. The group Ptah-Sokar-Osiris was not, properly speaking, an association of divine personages; rather, the group was a use of divine names to express complex divine functions having to do with the resurrection of the reconstituted body.

Certain groupings of four deities, such as the four sons of Horus, were the result of the association of two pairs: Amset and Hapi, Duamutef and Qebehsenuf. The heads of the four primordial divine generations—Re, Shu, Geb, and Osiris—were the origin of groups of rams that were receptacles of divine *ba*s, such as the Ram-of-Rams of Mendes, or of groups of crocodiles at Saft el-Henna. The number four is often related to the cardinal directions: the four supports of the sky, purification rites repeated four times, and so forth. In the Theban region, the group of four Montus resulted from the existence of four temples. Groups of seven, which are rarer, touch on magic. The Hathor goddesses who decided the fate of newborn children were seven in number, and in the Late Period, they were identified with various local forms of the goddess. The Hermopolitan Ogdoad was formed by doubling into couples the four personifications of the descriptive forces of the world of precreation (see p. 73).

Enneads and Divine Groups

The Ennead of Heliopolis was composed of the nine deities of the four primordial generations: (1) Atum; (2) Shu and Tefnut; (3) Geb and Nut; and (4) Osiris, Seth, Isis, and Nephthys (see p. 75). But "Ennead" was often a general term that designated a group of deities who existed in myth or cultic reality. There were seven such deities at Abydos. Two Enneads of fifteen deities dwelled at Karnak. The first, the "Great Ennead," was an assemblage of the major deities of the entire land, whereas the second, the "Lesser Ennead," served to associate local deities with the Great Ennead. The court of Amun thus comprised a *mabait*, a total of thirty deities. The number nine (i.e., three times three) was a sort of plural of plurals. Thus, the number of members in a group was more important than their identity. We have seen that the fourteen *ka*s and the seven *ba*s of Re received individual names only at a late date. The artificial character of these groupings resulted from their composition, and in most cases, the local "Enneads" surrounded the principal deity only on papyrus or, at best, on the walls of the temple.

For the ancient Egyptians, dividing the gods and goddesses into numerical sets was a way to impose order on the imaginary. The goal was not to enumerate its contents but, rather, to conceive a tidy structure with a reassuring logic.

Crowds of Deities and Their Leaders

As in the terrestrial realm, the subjects of the reigning god were there to acclaim him and loudly display the joy of the divine people in his presence. This role devolved on specialized anthropomorphic groups: the jackal-headed "*ba*s of Nekhen" and the falcon-headed "*ba*s of Pe" (Figure 17). These groups might have represented ancient sovereigns of Upper (Nekhen) and Lower (Pe) Egypt or ancient deities of these symbolic cities. Kneeling, the subjects beat their breasts with their fists and, with each blow, exclaimed a deep "Ha!" to greet the appearance of the sun. At their heads and turned toward them, the Meret-goddesses of the south and the north—the gracious directors of these noisy troupes of supporters—kept time by clapping their hands. Other groups played this role of acclaiming, enthusiastic crowds. Their appearance was varied (e.g., ram-headed, baboon-headed), but all these individuals remained anonymous. They were designated collectively by the name of the place where they were active: the Souls of the East, the Souls of the West, the Souls of Heliopolis who greeted and accompanied the sun, and so forth.

HIERARCHY AND RECRUITMENT OF DEITIES
Accession to Divinity

Private Persons Under certain conditions, the divine realm was accessible to ordinary mortals. The verb *senetjer* ("to make divine") desig-

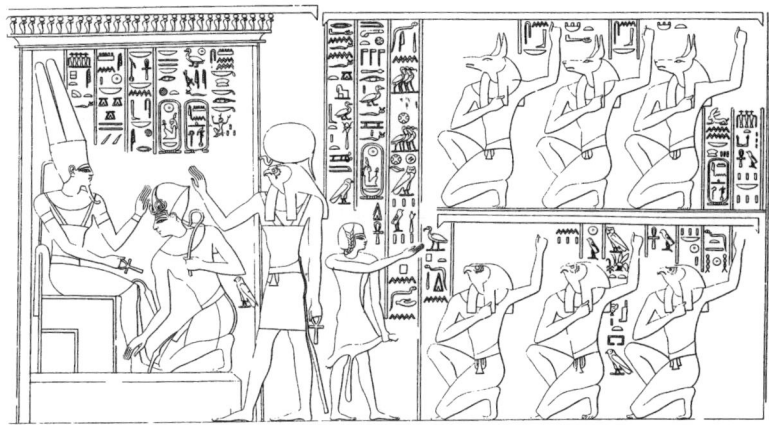

Figure 17. Left: King Amenophis III (*kneeling*) being crowned by Amun-Re (*left*) and the falcon-headed Horus. Top right: *Ba*s of Nekhen. Bottom right: *Ba*s of Pe. From the Temple of Luxor. After J.-F. Champollion, *Monuments de l'Égypte et de la Nubie*, vol. 4 (Paris, 1845), pl. CCCXLIV.

nates acts of purification that accompanied every change of status. In the Book of the Sky, the sun was purified when it passed below the horizon and entered the Duat. From Dynasty 11 on, by virtue of ritual, every deceased person became an Osiris—a divine being who inhabited the Duat and associated with deities and genies. Attainment of divine status with a cult recognized by all was not the result of a specific ritual; it was the social aspect of the deceased in the memory of the living that distinguished him in the afterlife. His faithful bore his name and hoped to attain the status of *imakhu* ("pensioner") in their company instead of the common wish to be an *imakhu* in the company of Osiris. At Saqqara, Paser of Dynasty 18 was attentive to the entreaties of his clientele: "Hear the supplications of (your) children and the personnel of your house [. . .] when you are called, you come immediately and roam your house on earth."[6] An overseer was a good candidate for deification, especially if his responsibilities extended to an entire city or region. Certain deceased foremen of teams of artisans became "perfect *akh*-spirits" and played the roles of intermediaries between their former subordinates and the divine realm.

Such was the case with Neferhotep of the Ramesside Period, deceased foreman of a team of workmen in the Valley of the Kings; he might have been assassinated by his successor Paneb—a very bad individual who was involved in a number of cases of theft, misappropriation of goods, and rape. Izi, governor of the nome of Edfu around 2460 B.C.E., became a "living god" after his death, and his cult was maintained at his tomb for five centuries. At Qau el-Kebir in Middle Egypt, the governors Ibu and Wakha also became the object of a cult. The governor of Elephantine under Pepy II—Pepinakht, surnamed Heqaib—enjoyed the same enviable fate, with the added privilege of a private chapel in the enclosure of Khnum. Kagemni, vizier of King Teti of Dynasty 6, was treated in the same fashion, undoubtedly because of his reputation as a wise judge. From the Late Period, we know of Nespamedu of Elephantine, who gave oracles, Bakennifi the Athribite, and Haremhab of Naukratis, not to mention the many "blessed ones" (*hesy*, literally, "praised ones"), such as Khay, the vizier of Ramesses II. But the renown of most of these personages remained purely local and relatively brief in duration.

The posthumous career of Imhotep, overseer of works under Djoser of Dynasty 3 and high priest of Heliopolis, was extraordinary. From the reign of Ramesses II on, he was considered to be god of scribes and physicians, the son of Ptah and Sakhmet. In the seventh century B.C.E., temples were consecrated to him; in the Greco-Roman Period, his cult grew to the point of making him the equivalent of Asclepius under the name Imuthes. Imhotep was the spouse of a woman named Good Year, an allusion to Sakhmet, protectress of the year. The name of his earthly mother, Khereduankh ("little children live") sounds like a programmatic name: the infant mortality rate was high in antiquity. His cult extended as far as Meroe in the Sudan, and it survived under various avatars down to the Christianization and Islamization of Egypt. Amenhotpe, son of Hapu, was a military man and overseer of works under Amenophis III, and he is presumed to have been responsible for such spectacular achievements as the erection of the colossi of Memnon. In the second century B.C.E., Amenhotpe received a joint cult with Imhotep in the temple of Deir el-Bahari at Thebes, which was converted into a place where oracles were given. Like Imhotep, he was a son of Ptah, but also of Thoth and of Seshat. His renown, however, scarcely extended beyond the region of Thebes.

Deified Kings The king's privileges as ritualist-intermediary made their appearance only after his coronation. They were not granted to him at birth, even though there is a sort of retroactive effect in the texts. The sacralization of political power depended more on the regalia (e.g., crowns, scepters, and royal images) than on the person of the king. Provided with these insignia and serving as officiant, the king was a *netjer-nefer*, but he became a full *netjer* only after death. At certain times, there was an attempt to extend the divinity of the royal office to the person of the sovereign (e.g., Ramesses II of Dynasty 19) or even the royal couple (e.g., Amenophis IV and Nefertiti of Dynasty 18). Examples of the cult of the deified king, whether dead or alive, are of two types. In the first category, the cult expressed the determined will of the political power. The motives were often politico-religious, and the form of the cult varied according to locale. Examples are the cults of statues of Ramesses II at Horbeit in Lower Egypt and of the living king in Nubia and the cult of dynastic founders carried out by their direct descendants (e.g., Dynasties 18, 19, 29, and 30) or their distant successors (e.g., the cult of Mentuhotpe under the Ramessides). In the Greco-Roman Period, Amenemhet III received a cult in the Faiyum, a region that had been developed during the Middle Kingdom.

In the second category, the cult was rendered to a sovereign who was wise and renowned in popular memory. Amenophis I, a king noted for his construction works, and his mother Ahmes-Nofretari, who were quite popular among necropolis workers, became the protectors and official intermediaries of the artisans and gentry of Thebes. Snofru was honored in the Sinai.

Divine Sovereignties

Mythic Royalties Coursing around the visible world since the first moments of creation, the sun was sovereign of the universe, the "master of all that exists and lives in the circuit of the disk." This solar kingship was the basis of royal ideology in Egypt, because Pharaoh, the image of Horus on earth, was the heir of Re. In major myths about divine founders, the god-kings who administered the land and organized humanity were Geb and Osiris. They exercised authority over the *pat*, the privileged subjects of the solar royalty. Beginning with the Middle Kingdom, the creator god's sovereignty extended beyond Egypt and encompassed all the "subjects" (*rekhyt*) of the universe. Ptah, "king of the sky," also dominated the Nubians, the Asiatics, and the Libyans. Transmission of power from one generation to the next was the principal goal of the myths of divine royalty.

According to a late account, Shu, son of Re-Harakhty, ruled at Memphis, but following a revolt, he distanced himself and ascended to the sky, leaving his companion Tefnut on earth. A royal god then violated Tefnut. Out of decency, the carver of the text left the name of the divine rapist blank, but it was Geb. This incest led to natural catastrophes but assured the legitimacy of Geb's power.

In the New Kingdom, patterns derived from the reality of terrestrial royalty were applied to divine sovereignty. The Royal Canon of Turin begins with a dynasty of eleven deities who reigned for a total of 7,714 years. Next, a dynasty of *akh*-spirits enabled a subtle transition between the "time of the gods" and human reigns, beginning with the anonymous Followers of Horus and then the historical kings of the Thinite Dynasty 1.[7]

The Rule of Amun Under Dynasty 21, divine sovereignty was invested with the trappings and procedures of human royalty. To express his will, Amun intervened directly in the real by rendering oracles, thus assuring the proper administration of his goods. Amun increasingly appeared to be a living god, present in his temple at Karnak, temporal regent of the universe and the divine realm and active counterpart of his primordial form buried at Medinet Habu (Djeme), whose funerary cult he assured in order to maintain the latent forces of the "first moment" (see p. 84). This tendency was already felt in the Ramesside Period.

To his faithful, Amun was in fact a king ruling over their destiny. On the lintels of the dwellings of the priests of Dynasty 21 at Karnak, the divine cartouche replaced the royal cartouche. Happy was a deceased person who, like Osirwer, could take along to his tomb a "royal decree for Osiris and all the gods around him" signed by Amun. A papyrus in the Cairo Museum preserves a copy of an oracular decree of Osiris that undertakes, among other things, to protect and nourish the inhabitants of the cities and nomes of Egypt.

Genies and Demons

As powers who acted in the realm of the inaccessible, genies and demons were *netjeru* ("gods"). But they were "poor relations" of the great figures of the pantheon, who benefited from the hospitality of a sanctuary in the real world. In the case of genies and demons, their function predominated over their personality. Their nature and appearance were concentrated in a name-function. They were an immediate and highly specialized response to a highly specific question. If we name the beings who guarded the gateways along the route traveled by the deceased through the arcana described in the Book of Two Ways, there pop up He-who-sticks-out-his-chest, Barker, He-with-the-repelling-face, or, descending into the disgusting, He-who-looks-backwards, and worse, He-who-eats-his-own-excrement.

Genies Genies were the product of specific, limited questions. A label such as geographic "personifications" suffices to characterize their domain. On the whole, genies' functions were essentially descriptive and enumerative, such as Hapy (the Nile), Mer (the canal of a nome), We (the agricultural land of a nome), Pehu (the marshes), Wadj-wer (the "great green," i.e., the sea).

Many genies had a more ambiguous status with regard to life in the countryside and what was produced there: Heb and Sekhet, god and goddess of hunting and the resources of the marshes; Hedjhotep and Tayt, god and goddess of weaving; Shesemu, god of the wine press, the oil press, and the perfume press; Merekhet, goddess of unguents; Menket and Tenmet, goddesses who brewed beer; Renenutet, goddess of the harvests; Neper, the grain god; Imenhy, the sacrificing god; Nefertem, the lotus god and incarnation of perfume; and Akhsu, the tree god.

Despite their specialization, some genies appear in the course of a myth rubbing elbows with major deities. We have already seen Hedjhotep interfering in the private life of Montu. At Memphis, promoted to the rank of divine child of Ptah and the terrifying Sakhmet, Nefertem took on bloodthirsty functions. The butcher gods Imenhy and Menhy seem to have had the benefit of residing at Asfun, near Edfu. Certain genies seem to have had a unique existence that was concentrated in an object, such as Peker, the sacred tree of Osiris at Abydos. Sometimes, even a major deity did not disdain to specialize, such as Hathor-of-the-sycamore, a tree venerated in one of the neighborhoods of Memphis.

Demons Demons and other dangerous beings were the price paid in the imaginary realm for people's fear in the face of their destiny. Death was a component of the world that was distributed equally to all. But the same was not the case with illness or other misfortunes, such as premature death and demon possession. Illness chose its victim; some were spared while others were affected. It was thus unjust, and Egyptians made great efforts to reconcile the apparent accident of illness with divine order. Sakhmet, the raging, bloodthirsty lion goddess, was just the right patroness for the redoubtable cohorts of demons who sowed misfortune on earth. Nekhbet, the goddess of El Kab, occasionally assumed the functions of Sakhmet, and like her, she would shoot seven arrows that wounded humanity. The "emissaries" of Sakhmet wandered the earth, striking blindly and causing "seasonal illnesses." Often, demons interceded in groups with disturbing names: "the ravishers," "the dead," "the powerful," "the enemies," "the prowlers," and "those of the night." These were *akh*-spirits who were particularly fond of the periphery of the organized world. They prowled about in the desert, the darkness, the waters, and in distant places. They were especially virulent in transitional

Figure 18. Cat, armed with a knife, slaying a serpent. After E. Naville, *Das ägyptische Totenbuch der XVIII. bis XX. Dynastie*, vol. 1 (Berlin, 1886), pl. XXX.

periods, such as during the five epagomenal days and when the deceased passed into the Duat. Demons were blind, dark, ugly, smelly, spoke incomprehensible gibberish, and loved to sow trouble. They were fond of traveling in groups of seven or multiples of seven. When artists ventured to represent them, they took on all sorts of human and animal forms (e.g., serpents, crocodiles, donkeys, dogs, cats, bulls, and rams) armed with knives (Figure 18).

When the end justified it, deities did not hesitate to employ demoniacal means. To assure their security, Osiris or Re would resort to a cohort of demon mercenaries. In a Ptolemaic story, Osiris sent the raging demons He-who-loves-war and Vengeance-of-Horus to fan the combative spirit of one of the protagonists of the tale. To protect oneself from the attacks of these redoubtable beings, it was necessary to be able to name them individually and to win over the good will of their generals—such as the sphinx Tutu (the Totoes of the Greeks)—or their divine protectress. Such was the goal of the Litanies of Sakhmet that were chanted in the great temples to assure the protection of the land for the coming year. Individuals were content to wear an amulet bearing the likeness of the goddess or the monsters she commanded.

6

Divine Functions

AGENTS OF CREATION

Like many peoples, the Egyptians wondered about the origins of the world. Day after day, year after year, the great cycles of nature lent rhythm to *neheh*-eternity; but surely there had been a first morning, a first inundation. What had the world of the "first moment" been like? What sort of mechanisms perpetuated it and operated the hidden face of the universe? This double question of the genesis (cosmogony) and the functioning (cosmology) of the universe was a major preoccupation of the ancient Egyptians. Their answers were numerous, for the more diverse the models, the more ways there were of acting on the imaginary through ritual.

Creation Stories

Whereas allusions to creation are frequent in texts of every period, mythological accounts—even partial ones—are rare. Taken together, they fall into three major groups.

The goal of the Coffin Texts was to introduce the deceased into the great cycles of the universe. Whether he had been a grandee or an ordinary bureaucrat, it was the deceased who would play the supreme role of the creator god, become Shu, or simply be present as an interested witness to the immense work of the ongoing creation. Different visions of the world of the "first moment" are expounded with a rigor approaching that of modern philosophical discourse. Theologians followed their trains of thought without attempting, at any cost, to reconstitute a single, fundamental myth for a cult place.

The same was not the case with the second group of mythological accounts, which were carved on the walls of the great temples of the Greco-Roman Period. These texts aim to establish the mythic origin of the local cults by means of ancient local traditions updated with teachings from the major religious centers. These highly composite and sometimes disparate accounts have the appearance of patchwork. In large part, they make use of puns on toponyms.

The final group of mythological accounts, magical texts, also belongs to the category of applied theology. Like the two preceding groups of texts, they draw their inspiration from ancient traditions, although their nature is essentially functional.

Cosmological Imagery

How did the Egyptians conceive of the physical world and its functioning? A ceiling from the cenotaph of Sethos I (1303–1290 B.C.E.) at Abydos bears an annotated representation of the world according to a tradition that, perhaps, dates back to the Middle Kingdom (Figure 19).

Here the Duat, the space of the nocturnal sun, is the interior of the body of Nut. The *akhet*-horizon, the place of transition and transformation, is the "place-of-becoming-efficient" (*akh*) or a sort of antechamber of the Duat. In fact, in the subterranean spaces of the pyramids, the funerary chamber called the *Duat* was preceded by a room called *Akhet*.

This representation of the world draws together metaphors of form (e.g., Nut is the vault of the sky) and metaphors of function (e.g., Nut is the mother of the sun). The rising sun was an infant being born, and certain descriptive terms evoke a veritable biological birth, although the creature being born in the sky is the winged scarab. To describe the reality of dawn, the hidden sun of the morning is represented at the feet of the goddess and not in the region of her genitals, from which the sun was supposed to emerge after having traversed the length of the goddess's body.

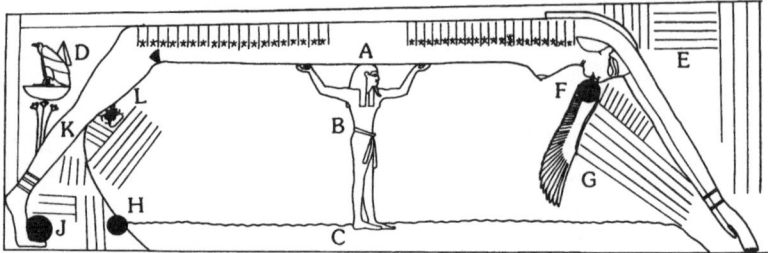

Figure 19. The universe according to the Book of Nut from the ceiling of the cenotaph of Sethos I at Abydos. **A:** Nut, the female celestial vault, her body studded with stars, stretches from east to west. **B:** Shu, space, father of Nut and Geb, supports Nut. **C:** The ground, sometimes represented by the recumbent god Geb. **D:** The goddess Nekhbet, protectress of the south. **E:** Description of the realm beyond creation. **F:** The setting sun, swallowed by Nut in the west. **G:** Description of the course of the sun: "entry by the majesty of this god in the first hour of dusk, he is still efficacious (*akh*) when he is received in the arms of his father Osiris," after which the sun god, purified, rests in the Duat. The next day, he "emerges on earth, in a very young and powerful form, as at the First Moment," and he transforms into the "great god of Edfu" (the sun soaring in the sky). He again enters the Duat via the mouth of Nut, followed by the stars, who "enter in his following and emerge after him." **H:** The sun at the first light of dawn: the disk "swimming in its redness" is still hidden. **J:** The sun rising from a horizon that is hidden from the visible horizon. **K:** The actual rising of the sun and its ascent into the sky: "emergence of the majesty of this god from the Duat . . . it is thus that he transforms and rises to the sky . . . and his heart and his might come into existence . . . and he comes into existence as when he came into existence in the world for the first time at the First Moment." **L:** The sun being born in the form of a winged scarab (*kheper*).

The World before Creation

Nut, Shu, and the sun delimited creation. Beyond it was an infinite liquid expanse, uniform and lightless, of which we are told that "the gods and *akh*-spirits" know nothing: "The upper part of the sky is uniform darkness. Its southern, northern, western, and eastern limits are unknown, they are fixed in the inertness of the primordial water, the light of the *Ba* (i.e., the sun) is absent from it" (see Figure 6, inscription above the back of Nut). This was the "fount of the gods."[1]

This realm beyond the universe had no name, for it was unorganized and thus the unnamed par excellence. When it was necessary to allude to this isomorphic, ideally homogeneous universe, it was called Nun—"inert liquid" or, perhaps better, "primordial waters."

In the Pyramid Texts, precreation was the simple nonexistence of the immediate world. Later, the cosmogonies of the Middle Kingdom described four entities representing the unorganized. The first two were deities: Nun ("water") and Hehu ("liquid space, the inundation"). The other two entities were qualifications of this universe: Keku ("darkness") and Tenmu ("disorder"). Other texts, also from the Middle Kingdom, speak of eight Hehu, but these are the supports of the sky, the creators of space who issued from Shu according to a tradition of Heliopolitan origin.

In the Hermopolitan tradition, as it was taken up and developed at Thebes, the creative forces that pervaded the unorganized were represented by four pairs of deities:

The Created		The Uncreated
Positive	Personifications	*Negative*
Solid	Nun and Naunet	Inert liquid
Delimited	Heh and Hauhet	Infinite space
Light	Kek and Kauket	Dark
Known	Amun and Amaunet	Unknown/hidden

These four entities are actually non-presences constituting a sort of negative description of the real. Opposed to the terra firma of our world is the liquid, inert, amorphous insubstantiality of Nun. The counterparts of our visible space, with its recognized boundaries and lit by the sun, are infinite space (Heh) and darkness (Kek). Finally, Amun, the "hidden one" or the "unknown," is the converse of that which is visible or knowable—in sum, that which peoples and fills the world. Later, a fifth couple was introduced: Niu and Niaut, personifications of the void. The uncreated world was the converse of a recognized space of terra firma, illumined by the sun and comprised of identifiable elements.

The cosmos of the Egyptians was thus a sort of bubble of air and light immersed in an inert and gloomy infinity of dark water.[2] The universe of precreation, ever-present, surrounded the cosmos and never ceased to threaten it. Waters that fell from the sky or surged up from the earth were reminders of the enveloping presence of Nun. Because all life emerged from him, Nun was a place of regeneration but also an emanation of the uncreated and, thus, a dangerous intrusion of the unorganized into the ordered world.

The Nun that was desired was that of the good inundation personified in the form of the genie Hapy: "You are he who appeases Nun and leads him in peace."[3] In the Book of the Earth, the solar barque—and thus the deceased—plunges into Nun, the source of life and rebirth.[4]

The Nun that was feared was that of the destructive waters of raging floods. That which ravaged the Theban region in the reign of Osorkon III of Dynasty 23 was described as a dangerous return to the original state: "Nun mounted [. . .] it came to beat the two mountainous sides, as at the time of origins."[5] The end of the world, which was rarely evoked, would be a return to the ever-latent primordial state: before the revolt of humankind, the All-Lord decided that "this land would return to the state of Nun."[6]

The Deities/Concepts of Creation

The deities/concepts of the very ancient Heliopolitan cosmogony were employed by many theological systems (Figure 20). They constituted the basis of a sort of common language.

The creator god—the being of the "first moment," "he who made himself," who fashioned the cosmos, "father of the gods"—was Atum. The nature of this being is contained in his name, which means "to complete, finish, achieve" but also "not to be." This etymological duality is indeed that of the creator god, who was an emanation of an undifferentiated universe but also the creator of the totality of this world. Atum was not only a deity/concept, but he was also a historical god who possessed an ancient cult center at Heliopolis.

From Atum, there emerged the first couple, Shu and Tefnut. The name *Shu* derives from a verb meaning "to be empty, dry," and his presence in the first moments of the cosmos is that of the space that separates the sky from the earth. From Shu emerged the liminal spaces above and below: Nut (the sky) and Geb (the earth). Nut and Geb formed a couple who were separated by their father. To establish a gendered symmetry with Nut and Geb, a goddess was attributed to Shu to be his consort: Tefnut, whose role was complex and often ambiguous. She was the atmosphere

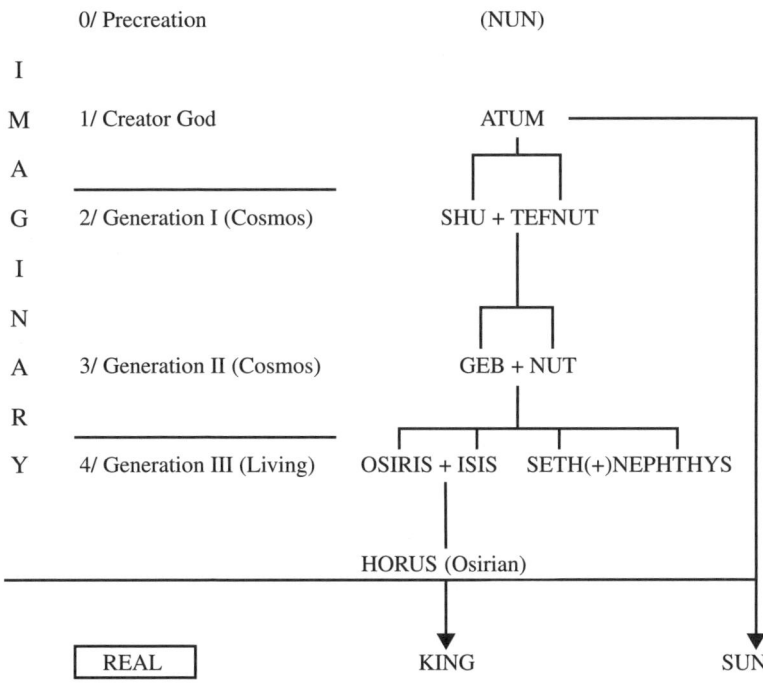

Figure 20. The Heliopolitan cosmogony.

of the netherworld in the Pyramid Texts, whereas in late periods, she incarnated a redoubtable destructive force that was sometimes ignited.

With these five deities, the framework of the world of creation was in place. The third generation that issued from Atum symbolized the world of the living and its social order. This generation was made up of antagonistic elements: Osiris, the wise sovereign, was opposed to Seth, brute force, who ruled over the untamed zones of the world. Osiris' wife Isis was the divine mother, and after a fashion, the couple represented the human race. Nephthys, sister and companion of Osiris, had a less conspicuous role in the theology of Heliopolis, but to maintain the symmetry of couples and antagonistic entities, she was sometimes considered to be the wife of Seth. Unlike Isis, Nephthys was not a mother. These deities, who fell victim to the human fate that was death, were able to conquer eternity, the ultimate human hope: individual salvation was connected with Osiris, who ruled the Duat, whereas the collective survival of human society depended on the survival of an heir—a function assumed by the child Horus, son of Isis.

We may be surprised by the absence of Re and Horus from the Heliopolitan Ennead, strictly speaking. This is because these important figures belonged to human time: the former was the daily sun, whereas the latter was the principle of kingship, which ordered the human realm.

In the cosmologies, four common terms designated the sun. *Re* was the name of a state, designating the heavenly body in the plenitude of its zenith. *Atum* was the name of the waning, transitory state at dusk. *Khepri*, the name of the waxing, transitory state, characterized the sun as it rose and climbed in continuous transformation toward the zenith. Finally, *Aten* was the name of the material sun, the luminous disk that crossed the sky.

Horus, the son and heir of Osiris, whom Kurt Sethe called the "tenth god of the Ennead," was an essentially royal deity, legitimated by the inheritance of his father Osiris. His emblematic image, the falcon, like his name *Hor* ("distant one"), expressed the distance of the solar deity.

COSMOGONIC PROCEDURES

The Creator and the Will to Create

The Egyptians were not content with the image of the creator, the primordial monad splendid and glorious in his sublime and inexplicable creative solitude. At an early date, they speculated on the causes of the act of creation. According to spell 75 of the Coffin Texts, the creator god, alone in the inert expanse of Nun, conceived of Shu "in his heart" before proceeding to the act of creating him. Creation was thus part of a design, a deliberate intention of the creator. In the cosmogony of immaterial space, the first cause was none other than the principle of life (*ankh*), itself issued from the creator: "Atum said to Nun, 'It is my son Life who has lifted my heart.'" Thus is forged a causal link adding a stimulating element of the creative act to the fact of an emanation from the creator.

Because creation was the consequence of a masculine, solitary sexual act, the nature of the creator's stimulation was not especially philosophical. In this particular metaphorical field, the erotic means of the masturbating god was a feminine entity. The most common entity was Hathor, mistress of love and pleasure, the opposite of Isis, the sage wife and mother. In this role, Hathor assumed the form of a goddess with four faces (Hathor Quadrifrons).[7]

In Theban cosmogony, Hathor was the "mistress of the seed that emerged from him" (i.e., from the primordial, ithyphallic Amun). At Heliopolis, two goddesses, Iusaas and Nebethetepet, were often identified as the "hand of the god" (i.e., the hand of the creator god carrying out his solitary act). The name *Iusaas* means "when she comes, she is large"—a metaphor that applies to the inundation and to other natural or physiologic phenomena. *Nebethetepet* can be translated as "mistress of calming." Finally, Tefnut, daughter of Atum, was also a "hand of the god"; she shared the title with the Divine Adoratrices of Amun at Karnak, wives of the ithyphallic god. A particularly undisciplined priest at Elephantine had his wife come to him during the night of mourning for Osiris. Quite inebriated, he declared shamelessly and before witnesses, "Tefnut, no goddess can measure up to her!" This inglorious act earned him a day in court.[8]

The Primeval Mound, Spitting, and Masturbation

The Primeval Mound was the transposition into the imaginary realm of the origins of the annual spectacle of bits of land emerging from the water as the inundation ebbed. In the Pyramid Texts, Atum, addressed by his name Khepri, appears on this mound, which was the first solid element in the cosmos.

The appearance (*weben*) of the Primeval Mound and of a mythic bird called *Benu* ("lord of the *benben*-stone") is described by means of a word play on the root *ben* ("to become swollen; to be full, round") and its various derivatives (e.g., "to point upward, ball, womb, expanding curve, to come, high point," and so forth).

Next, the text depicts the creator god at work: "You spat (*ishesh*) what was Shu, you sputtered what was Tefnut."[9] Elsewhere in the same collection of spells, the creation of the first couple by a solitary being is inspired by the model of human generation: "He took his penis in his fist and had an orgasm by means of it, and the two twins were born."[10] Thus, the deities of the Ennead were derived from the substance of Atum.

Immaterial Space

In spells 75–80, the Coffin Texts develop a spatial vision of the universe and its creation.[11] According to spell 75, Shu, a metaphor for space, developed within the very body of the creator god: "I sprung up in his legs, I came into existence in his arms, I created space in his body." Spell 76 specifies the immateriality of the birth of Shu: "I was neither created in a body, nor tied together in an egg, nor conceived in a womb; my father Atum spat me out in a spitting of his mouth." Separating what was above from what was below, Shu created the space of his father Atum. In this way, he enabled the creation of the sun and thus the development of time. By way of a consequence, Shu was also *neheh*-eternity.

Word, Thought, Artisan

The process of creation was not always a physical emanation from the creator god. The oral manifestation of his will sufficed: "many are the transformations (*kheperu*) that issued from my mouth."[12] This is the principle of "creative utterance." But the Egyptians knew that the efficacious word was but a moment in a complex process. First, there was thought (conception), and then there was speech and the passage from thought to reality. Beginning in the Coffin Texts, Ptah the creator conceived (*sia*) "in his body" and pronounced (*hu*) "with his mouth."[13]

A block of black granite stemming from Memphis and known as the Shabaka Stone (Dynasty 25, 715–701 B.C.E.) bears a copy of an ancient papyrus "found by his majesty [. . .] eaten by worms" and whose content was "unknown from beginning to end." It was long thought that the original papyrus dated back to the Old Kingdom, but it is now agreed that its composition could not have occurred earlier than the reign of Ramesses II. In the system expounded in this document, the twin concepts of thought and speech are symbolized by the human organs that are their seat: the heart (*haty*) and the tongue (*nes*). "Heart and tongue control all limbs . . . and every mouth of all the gods, all people, all animals, every living, creeping thing, thinking (*kaa*) and pronouncing everything they desire." Another passage details the role of the heart as a conduit of information from the three senses (i.e., sight, hearing, and smell), causing "the emergence of every conclusion," although it is by means of the tongue that "the thoughts (*kaa*) of the heart are passed on."[14]

Scholars have thought that the Shabaka Stone reflects the syncretistic ambition of Ptah of Memphis and his clergy: Ptah, in his form of Ta-tenen ("the rising land"), "gave birth to the gods" and organized the land. Recent research, however, has shown that "Ptah" and "heart and tongue" are not divine personages, but rather philosophical terms designating the intellectual creative process. *Ptah* is the name of the tool employed by the creator god. Thus, according to the Memphite theologians, at the beginning of creation, the "principle of Ptah" (heart and tongue) was preexistent.

This creative process was directly related to the personality of the old Memphite god Ptah, the divine artisan and patron of sculptors and masons. Ptah presided over the "Mansions of Gold"—the workshops where the artisan-priests of ancient times fashioned the precious images of the deities. The conception of a project by forethought (*kaa*) and its subsequent realization through intelligible expression were part of the daily life of artisans.

Khnum of Esna, the divine potter, was also an artisan-god "who turned gods and modeled humans and animals."[15] In the myth of the divine birth of Amenophis III, however, he merely fashioned the child conceived by Amun.

Marsh, Flower, Egg, Mud

The blue lotus—that elegant water lily that opens in the morning and closes in the evening, born of moisture and emanating a pleasant scent—was an ideal figure for myths of creation. This characteristic image of the Hermopolitan system, already known in the Old Kingdom, blossomed in the New Kingdom.

In the hidden recesses of Nun, in a place called the Great Lake, which was traditionally located in Hermopolis, the Great Lotus appeared of its own accord, emerging from the surface of the water to the acclamations of the four primordial couples. Spreading its petals, the flower revealed the sun in the form of an infant. The child opened his eyes, separating night from day: "You chased away the clouds, you repelled the darkness, you illuminated the Two Lands."[16]

At Edfu, we find a typical image of the delta landscape. A cluster of rushes and vegetal debris floats on the surface of Nun. A mythic falcon, a royal bird, soars and circles above this tiny island of plants and then alights on it. Then, a superior divine being manifests his will in the form of a gigantic bird and appoints the falcon as "lord of the universe."[17]

The reproductive model of creatures that lay eggs also inspired the Egyptians. This tradition was also linked to Hermopolis, but we have no connected account of this system of creation, assuming such an account ever existed. According to certain formulations in the Coffin Texts, this egg emerged from a mythical bird called the Great Honker. Texts from the New Kingdom have the sun emerge from a mysterious egg "like the child of the Eight." Conversely, according to later texts, the Eight emerged from an egg that was created and inseminated by Ptah. Elsewhere, the egg is said to have contained breath—a description made, without doubt, by phonetic analogy between the words for egg (*suhe*) and breath (*suh*).

A text from the Roman Period, recently discovered at Koptos, makes use of an inorganic model: the world emerges from the coils of the serpent Irto ("he who makes the earth") in the form of a primordial mass called *benu*. The latter splits open, spilling out fertile soil in a sort of mudslide. Geb, the chthonic being par excellence, is the primordial power animating this earthy cosmogony.

THE ORGANIZATION OF THE UNIVERSE
Golden Age and Revolt

The world was created, but it had to be organized. From the unique being of the "first moment," there emerged the infinite diversity of our universe. The oldest texts are rather discreet concerning this phase of creation. Before the gods and goddesses, the creator god made humankind (*remetj*), which emerged from his tears (*remyt*). The Instruction for Merikare (*c.* 2100 B.C.E.) describes a creation that is ordered entirely for the welfare of humanity: "He created sky and earth for them, he repelled the Greedy One of the waters . . . he made plants for them, and beasts and birds and fish to nourish them."[18] The Shabaka Stone expounds the work of Ptah-Tanen, the creator/organizer who succeeded the creator god and set in place the framework of liturgical society—deities, cities, and nomes—placing the gods and goddesses in their sanctuaries.

In the Middle Kingdom, but especially beginning with the New Kingdom, myths involved deities in a history in the imaginary realm, outside of real time, but whose models were drawn from the political and social reality of the land. The chief god was a solar sovereign who caused "Maat, daughter of Re" to rule on earth; this goddess was the incarnation of the principles of social cohesion.

Abundance, security, and comfort reigned in the time of the Primeval Ones: "Maat had come from the sky [. . .]. The land was flooded and bellies were full, there was no famine in the land [. . .], walls were not collapsed, stings did not prick, the crocodile did not attack, and serpents did not bite."

But the delights of this ideal reign, which are in fact rarely described, scarcely lasted. Accounts of the revolt of humankind, which are more frequent, introduce the violence of reality into the myth. Even the compassionate creator god of the Instruction for Merikare conducted himself like a brutal sovereign: "He killed his enemies and punished his children, for they fomented revolt." The motives for the uprising are not stated. This was not a case of an organized rebellion against authority, accompanied by a list of demands but, rather, acts of indiscipline toward Maat: people did not act according to the principle of social order, but rather abandoned themselves to their unfortunate natural passions. Anarchy reigned and disorder (*isfet*, the opposite of Maat) gained the upper hand: "They cried out, they spread disorder, they committed murder, they created imprisonment."[19] In origin myths, the revolt was the justification for the divine combat—a campaign of suppression that made the sanctuaries of Egypt into so many memorials of terrible battles between the powerful divine authority, often Horian, and his enemies. These victorious combats attest to the efficacy of the local theologies over the forces of disorder.

At Edfu, the Myth of Horus is an account of punitive combats treated after the fashion of history.[20] In year 363 (a magical number) of the reign of King Re-Horus-of-the-Two-Horizons, revolt broke out in Lower Nubia. Re dispatched Horus of Behdet in the form of the winged sun disk. Blinded, the enemies panicked and killed one another. Before the transfixed bodies, Thoth said, "Horus has harpooned (*djeba*) them," and "that is why Horus is called Horus of Edfu (*Djeba*) down to our day." In this manner, the text enumerates and describes a long series of divine combats that took Re and his champion Horus from the Sudan to the sea, justifying the etymologies of dozens of more or less Horian toponyms.

We must draw a distinction between the theme of punitive combat and that of primordial combat—the image of the battle of the organizing force against opposing forces stemming from Nun. The latter often were in the guise of a serpent.

At Edfu, the falcon had scarcely taken possession of the isle of vegetation when a serpent emerged from chaos and attacked him. The creator god then fashioned four armed creatures: a bird of prey, a lion, a serpent, and a bull. These genies, who represented the four basic groups of the animal kingdom (i.e., birds, carnivores, reptiles, and herbivores), multiplied, and from each of them, there emerged fourteen combative forms. Along with their squadron leaders, this company of guardians at Edfu totaled sixty (4 × 15) *sauensen* ("protection is theirs"). They formed a protective square around the creator god. In the real world, they were always present in the form of the enclosure wall of the temple, which was considered to be their emanation.

At Esna, the theme of primordial combat was mixed with that of punitive combat. This very late cosmogony associated diverse traditions of varied origins in a disparate relationship. The general structure of the account consists of five major sections: the initial manifestation of the goddess Neith, the creator; the birth of the sun; the birth of Apopis and the revolt; the punitive journey of Mehet-weret and her Seven Words; and the institution of the festivals of Esna and Sais. Between these moments of action, glosses and commentaries are interposed to justify the local religious toponymy and enable the intervention of all the divine forms known to tradition.

At the beginning of the account, Neith, "father of fathers, mother of mothers," appears "by herself" in Nun. She assumes the appearance of a cow, and then, without our knowing why, she turns into a lates-fish. Light streams from her eyes just before she beaches on the first solid land "in the midst of the initial waters." She utters creative words that furnish a cosmogonic etymology not only for the sacred places of Latopolis (Esna), but also for their equivalents at Sais, for Esna was the Sais of Upper Egypt. The serpent Apopis is born of Neith's spittle and engages in combat. Finally, toward the end of the account, the goddess turns into the cow called the Great Swimmer (Mehet-weret). Along with her son Re, the sun between her horns, she undertakes a punitive journey of four months' duration, slaughtering her enemies wherever they were to be found.

To lend some coherence to this account, which was more than disparate, the theologians of Latopolis had the idea of personalizing the creative words that Neith-Mehet-weret speaks during the course of the story. These were the "Seven Speeches of Mehet-weret." After playing their founding roles, these seven divine "speeches" died and were buried in the sacred necropolis of Esna.

The Destiny of the Creator God and the Dead Gods

Once creation had been completed and the universe had been organized, the forces of the "first moment" were laid to rest. But they were present in the real world, resting in the sacred necropolis, where a cult was rendered to them by the local deity, who was their own living form in the temple.

Around the seventh century B.C.E., the "veritable *ba* who is in Thebes" rested in the small temple of Medinet Habu, an ancient cult place in the Theban necropolis. Later texts inform us that this mysterious *ba* was surrounded by the Ogdoad of Hermopolis—"father of fathers, the lords of the mound of Djeme, the Primeval Ones of the gods." Beginning with the eleventh century B.C.E., Amun of Opet would visit this sanctuary to "offer water to the great living *ba*s who rest in the place United-with-Eternity." Amun of Opet was the primordial, procreative form of Amun residing in the temple of Luxor, the "place of the first moment" and of the royal birth. This libation, which was made every ten days (the "decade ritual"), was an ancient funerary ritual intended to refresh the deceased. Texts of the Ptolemaic Period enable us to reconstruct the cosmogonic myth of Thebes that formed the basis of the "decade" rites of Djeme according to the local theologians of the third and second centuries B.C.E.[21]

The Primeval Gods were "fashioned in Nun" by "Tanen in the Southern Opet (i.e., the temple of Luxor)," and they were also the children of Irto, the serpent that created the world. After their birth, they swam north until they reached the Lake of Fire, the primordial pond of Hermopolis, where they pulled themselves up onto an elevation. There, in their midst, "the lotus of Re emerged, and light burst forth after the darkness in its name of Amun." Once this act of enlightenment was accomplished, they returned to their place of origin and "rested in their Nun at Djeme," where "they received the Duat of Kematef." The meaning of the name of the serpent Kematef—"He-who-has-completed-his-time"—recalls that of Atum, his equivalent at Heliopolis. Like the serpent Irto, his counterpart at the beginning of creation, Kematef was a manifestation of Amun, the Great *Ba* of Egypt.

The choice of Hermopolitan metaphors to describe the birth of the sun in a myth of Amun led to the strange aquatic journey to Hermopolis on the part of the Ogdoad. The heterogeneity of the theological sources, consisting in large part of Memphite, Heliopolitan, and Hermopolitan components, determined the unfolding of the story.

In the inner recesses of their tomb, these beings from the beginning of time were not inactive: they saw, they heard, and as creatures of Nun, they assured the periodic return of the inundation. Amun of Opet's visit to Djeme every ten days in the form of a veiled statue of the ithyphallic god profited all the deceased in the necropolis[22]; other deities also derived benefit from this theology of the dead gods.

Khons the Elder celebrated a daily cult for the dead gods of Djeme.[23] In reality, the ritual was carried out in a chapel at Karnak, the local substitute for the sanctuary at Medinet Habu. As for Montu, he traveled to Djeme to honor the dead gods on the twenty-sixth day of the month of Khoiak under the name of Montu-Osiris-Atum.[24] In the desert of Edfu, there rested the bodies of a group of nine local deities. They remained "breathing in life" in their tomb, which was visited annually by Horus of Edfu and Hathor of Dendara. The dead form of Min-Osiris rested in the necropolis of Koptos, where every ten days it received a thirst-quenching visit from the veiled image of Min. Certain deceased persons at Koptos had the special privilege of being buried in the temple forecourt, so that they might receive their sanctifying libation from the god himself. They were given the title "blessed" (*hesy*)—a term that would come to mean "drowned ones" in Coptic.[25] These blessed ones are known from other cities in Egypt as well.

Creator gods rested, deities animated the universe, regal gods reigned, and Pharaoh maintained the cults. Eternity would have been peaceful, had there not been fomenters of trouble.

Divine Fomenters of Trouble

It happened that the world did not turn exactly according to divine order. A number of deities were involved in this drama, playing the role of rogue in the mythical maneuvers.

The serpent Apopis was a liminal being, an intrusion of primordial disorganization into the organized universe, and one of the forces of nonexistence that disturbed the existing. If famine swept the land, it was because the barque of Re had run aground on the "sandbank of the serpent Apopis."

Though Seth was every bit as brutal and dangerous as Apopis, he was one of the elements of creation. He was a disordered element, to be sure—the scorching wind blowing across the desert, the eternal belligerent and rival of Horus—but he figured honorably in the divine company. This blind and destructive energy could be used to good ends. Re had recourse to Seth to combat the monster Apopis (Figure 21).

Figure 21. Seth battling Apopis.

In sum, the fomenters of trouble fell into two categories. On one hand, there was the troublemaker and necessary evil: the aggressive Seth and his various avatars (e.g., crocodiles, serpents, scorpions, and donkeys). On the other hand, there was the monster Apopis and his transformations (e.g., the serpents Nehaher, Nik, and Rik). Mortal enemy of Re, Apopis was the nihilist of the ultimate catastrophe. For him, it was not a question of disturbing the cosmos but of abolishing it. Seth was disorder, but Apopis was the end of all order!

In the daily practice of their imaginary realm, the Egyptians were obliged to find ways to deal with these beings. Taken hostage by the terrifying beings of the Duat, they maintained equivocal relations with their torturers. Directly confronting the demons of the netherworld, deceased persons addressed them, greeting them and asking for their protection. Even the evil genie Nehaher would forget his cosmic function and grant his protection; in a crypt of the temple of Dendara, he is called "master of the rage that swallows the enemies of Re."[26]

Such reversals were not rare among genies and demons. The repugnant tortoise Wenemhuaat ("eater of decay") ended his career as an efficacious protector and dispenser of the inundation.[27] The seventy-four demons with strange names (e.g., Blazing-in-the-ground, He-of-the-cauldron, and He-who-cries) who threatened the route of the sun's course became seventy-four forms of Re.[28]

SPECIAL FUNCTIONS

Complex Functions: The Example of Osiris

The world was not a simple superimposition of primary and distant cosmic forces. As a living being, a person experienced the immediate, daily proximity of complex phenomena: life and death, the cycles of vegetation, the renewal of the generations, and the equilibrium of social groups. Descriptions of these mechanisms in the ideal realm of the imaginary employed images, personages, and, in particular, complex mythical sequences. Perhaps Re could do without a mythic story, inasmuch as his glorious, daily regality was obvious, but this was not the case with Osiris, the central figure in a set of dramas whose necessary exposition had recourse to numerous divine actors.

Strictly speaking, there was no single written and codified myth of Osiris. As needed, texts drew on a series of sequences linked to the themes of the myth: the royal rule of Osiris, his violent death, the mourning over him, the safeguarding of his body, his posthumous heir, his resurrection, the legal proceeding, his revenge, and so forth. The details of the episodes were varied: violence, illness, drowning for the assassin, the lamentations of Isis and Nephthys, the falling of leaves, low water to symbolize the mourning for him, the magic of Isis, germination symbolizing his resurrection, and so forth.

From the Pyramid Texts on, more than one series of mythic episodes were superimposed. According to one of them, Osiris was assassinated by his brother Seth, and the magic of Isis and Nephthys made it possible to restore him to life. The child Horus was born of a postmortem conception. The god was avenged, and Seth was condemned by the divine tribunal, which recognized Osiris's paternity. The other episode relates the eternal combat between Horus and Seth to win sovereignty over Egypt. In their conflict with one another, the two gods were well suited to play the roles of the avenging son and the assassin.

According to their intended goal, writers would reach into the "Osiriana" and choose a particular episode in a particular tradition according to the specifics of the ritual context of the document they were composing.

Plutarch, who left a connected, highly detailed version of the myth, puts the reader on guard: this account is only an "image of a certain truth that reflects a single thought in different milieus," and if these fictions risk being believed, it is better "to reject them by spitting and rinsing one's mouth." The episodes in Plutarch's account are of pharaonic origin, but the whole is a disparate patchwork whose material is drawn from the Osiriana accessible to the Greeks. Thus, it is necessary to extract from the myth that which constitutes its essence: Osiris, a very ancient royal god, expresses all the recurrent forces of humanity (e.g., death and resurrection), of society (e.g., inheritance and legitimacy), of the world (e.g., vegetation and the Nile), and by extension, of the cosmos (e.g., moon and light).

The Animation of Complex Functions

Osiris's "ana" made it possible to describe and account for various recurrent mechanisms. The Egyptians pondered the nature of the force that, beyond the metaphors proper to Osiris and the deities associated with him, animated this recurrence. For the Theban theologians of the first millennium B.C.E., this hidden cause animating (among other things) the myth of Osiris was Amun. In the temple of Opet at Karnak, a strange composite bird, ithyphallic and bearing the head of Amun, hovers over the renascent Osiris. It is "Amun-Re, the venerable *ba* of Osiris." This is not a matter of the equivalence— much less an assimilation or fusion— of the two deities but, rather, the description of a hierarchized theological structure.

A scene depicted on the wall of the crypt represents the ten *ba*s of Amun striding toward the image of Osiris and extending to him a chain made up of hieroglyphs for "life" (Figure 22). Each *ba* of Amun animates a sector of the universe. From the top left, the first is "Amun, the *ba* who is in his right eye" (the sun), and the second is "Amun, the *ba* who is in his left eye" (the moon). Described with the aid of appropriate metaphors, there follow breath and space (*ba* 3), water (*ba* 4), fire (*ba* 5), humanity (the royal *ka*, *ba* 6), large and small cattle (*ba* 7), flying creatures (*ba* 8), aquatic creatures (*ba* 9), and the forces of plant growth (the serpent Provider-of-*ka*s, *ba* 10).

Immanence and Transcendence

In Chapter 200 of Papyrus Leiden I 350 from the Ramesside Period, Amun is the "prodigious god, rich in transformations." His *ba* is present in the "distant sky," the Duat, and the nearer sky, whereas his body is in the necropolis, and "his statue is in Heliopolis of the south (i.e., Thebes)."[29] Amun's immanence is dazzling. Without a transition, the text paradoxically continues: "Unique is Amun . . . who conceals himself from the gods, his aspect is unknown, he is more distant than the distant sky, deeper than the Duat . . ., the gods do not know his true form . . . no god can invoke him." This is a god who is distanced from his creation, exterior to the world and thus transcendent, unknowable, without a cult, and unapproachable. This text is not unique, and Ramesside hymns are rich in descriptions of the unique and distant solar deity.[30] According to this passage of the hymn, the cultivated scribes of the Ramesside Period admitted the idea of a transcendent, unique god similar to that of the great monotheistic systems. But how is one to resolve the difficulty of the jux-

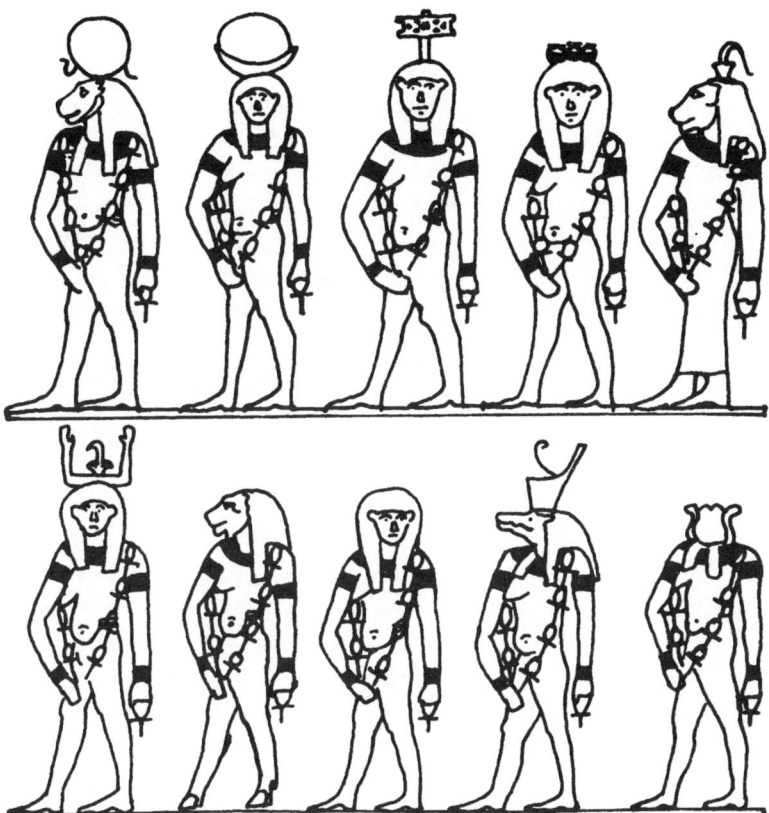

Figure 22. The ten *ba*s of Amun.

taposition of two such opposed concepts? The answer lies, we believe, in the concept of precreation, which is characteristic of Egyptian cosmology. For the Ramesside theologians, Amun was transcendent in his capacity of preexisting creator, as the unique one of the "first moment," but within his creation, Amun was immanent![31] As for the infinite multitude of gods and goddesses, even though they are emanations of Amun in this system, they also possessed an existence of their own, and we cannot speak of monotheism. Precreation, creation, and the living world formed an indissociable and ever-present whole.

Amenophis IV and Atenism

Amenophis IV (1352–1338 B.C.E.) is commonly presented as a mystic and a pacifistic sovereign, the inspired prophet of a state-supported monotheism. From the beginning of his reign, in fact, everywhere in Egypt, the young king founded a solar cult dedicated to the falcon-headed god "Harakhty-who-rejoices-in-the-horizon-in-his-name-of-'Light-which-is-in-the-disk.'" He made this god the basis of a new theology of royalty that was characterized by the image of the radiant sun disk, Aten. In the hymns addressed to the Aten ("Disk"), the deity was a god of love:

> Your rays, they touch everyone . . . you fill the Two Lands with your love, people live when you rise for them . . . you have caused that the sky be distant that you might rise in it to gaze upon your creation, you are unique, but there are a million lives in you.[32]

In year 6 of his reign, Amenophis IV took the name Akhenaten and founded Akhetaten (Tell el-Amarna), a new city dedicated to his god, but his experiment came to naught. The archaeological traces of a persecution of the name of Amun—the sign of a period of extreme radicalism in the state-supported Aten system—has caused some to think that the battle between Amun and Aten was one between an obscurantist polytheism and an enlightened monotheism. If we add to these facts the beauty of the king's wife, Nefertiti, the free elegance of the art of this period, and the bitterness of his ultimate failure, we have all the ingredients to make a contemporary myth out of this ancient king. In fact, this theology went back at least two reigns before Amenophis IV. It was based on the principle of the distance of the sun god. Akhenaten's god was not Aten (the "Disk"), but the entity with an unknown name who manifested himself in the disk as the "Light-which-is-in-the-disk." He was a divine sovereign, and his protocol was written in a double cartouche, whereas the king was his counterpart on earth. Like the transcendence and immanence of Amun, Atenism was not basically incompatible with the classical divine polysemy. There are a number of examples of the cohabitation of the two systems: Akhenaten taught that his god possessed knowledge of the *iru*-forms of each god and goddess; there was a list of the gods of Egypt on a wall of the Aten temple at Karnak, which was next to the temple of Amun; the queen was the earthly image of Hathor[33]; and so forth. Akhenaten was an authoritarian monarch, and we now know that military campaigns took place during his reign. A recently discovered relief at Karnak shows the small, beneficent hands of the Disk holding out a scimitar and a mace to the king as he smites a foreign enemy.[34] The theology of Aten was purely phenomenological, describing the blessings bestowed by the heavenly body in a *creatio continua* that was daily and immediate.[35] There was no cosmogony, no geography of the imaginary realm. But unlike Amun's theologians in the Ramesside Period, Amenophis IV was not content to write and meditate. By substituting his own person and that of his queen for the ancient cult statues in a curious combination of solar and classical ritual principles (see pp. 34 and 95), he tried to give a tangible, terrestrial, and royal reality to a philosophy.

7

The Gods and the Human Realm

MEANS OF COMMUNICATION

Shu, the space of communication, "transmits the words of He-who-came-into-being-by-himself to his multitude."[1] Divine *ba*s permeated the world and inhabited the cult statues. But for the individual, these means of collective communication, though vital and effective, were insufficient. Deities and humans thus sought more direct means of communication to enable the former to express their will and the latter to make their prayers heard.

From the Divine Realm to the Human

When a deity wished to intervene directly, he could assume a human disguise and act as an *akh*-spirit. But, as we have seen, this rarely happened. The apparition of a god in a dream was more frequent, although it was reserved for persons of royal blood. Deities played only a minor role in the "dream books" consulted by ordinary people.

Young Prince Tuthmosis, dozing at the feet of the Great Sphinx at Giza, was visited by the god Harmakhis, who came to request that the prince free the deity's effigy from the sand that was covering it.[2] In the later periods of Egyptian history, certain private individuals received advice directly from a deity—an example being Sematawytefnakhte, the personal physician of Darius III. The god Harsaphes personally advised him to desert from the Persian army after its defeat at Arbela near Nineveh and to return to Herakleopolis. Harsaphes protected the physician-collaborator throughout his perilous journey.[3]

Later, undoubtedly under Greek influence, healing gods like Imhotep and Amenhotpe son of Hapu deigned to appear to patients who came to seek a cure for their maladies by spending a night under the porticos of their temples. In general, however, Egyptians feared direct confrontation with beings from the imaginary realm. Faced with the apparition (though charming) of a nude goddess in the vicinity of a pond, the shepherd of a Middle Kingdom story was terrified: his hair stood on end, and fear spread through his limbs.[4]

Magical texts put the conjuror on guard against the danger of seeing demons: "If living beings were to see him, they would die and be set on fire."[5] But this redoubtable demon, the paniconic Bes (Figure 23)—a veritable war machine, a magical creature with seven faces, eight wings, and

Figure 23. Paniconic Bes. Vignette from a magical papyrus. Brooklyn Museum 47.218.156 a–c. Photograph courtesy of the Brooklyn Museum of Art, Collection of Charles Edwin Wilbour, gift of the Estate of Ms. Theodora Wilbour.

millions of horns—was committed to the good cause of protecting the deceased and the king. To intervene in the lives of ordinary people, deities made use of the fearsome cohorts of the "emissaries" of Sakhmet, the goddess of all dangers (see pp. 68, 97, 104, and 111) or, worse still, wandering spirits who were capable of springing up anywhere. Addressed to an individual at the initiative of a deity, the message could announce only the inevitable: "The divine message (of Amun), it is destined to kill or to make live."[6]

Deities had other means of imparting information to humans. We have seen sovereign deities making decrees. Wise gods wrote books that humans would discover by chance while searching through a temple. Events that were natural but remarkable—or even extraordinary—could be signs of divine will, of the many *bia*-miracles granted to humans by the divine.

Chapter 30 of the Book of the Dead, written by Thoth himself, was found by Prince Djedefhor.[7] Sometimes a deity would appear in a dream to reveal the location of a precious roll of papyrus or demand a Greek translation of one of his works, as in the case of the Aretalogy of Imuthes. One night, a book of magic fell from the sky at the temple of Isis in Koptos. In the mining area of the Wadi Hammamat, a gazelle gave birth and thus revealed to Mentuhotpe's quarrymen the block of stone that would be the cover of his majesty's sarcophagus.[8]

One day, during a ceremony in the temple of Amun, the barque of Amun veered from its route, moved by an irresistible force, and came to a halt before Prince Tuthmosis, the future Tuthmosis III.[9] By means of this spontaneous oracle, Amun designated the sovereign whom he wished to reign. Ordeals, though attested in mythic accounts,[10] were not a common practice in Egypt.

From Humans to the Divine

People had three ways to communicate with the divine: cult, consulting oracles,[11] and personal prayer. Cult was carried out according to a liturgical calendar that took into account only the moments of natural cycles, both divine and royal. Words and acts were addressed to a deity through the mediation of a statue charged with the divine *ba*. By means of oracles, persons would directly question deities, drawing them into the time of the real. If the person was a sovereign, the deity could speak to him directly.

Tuthmosis IV, advised of an uprising in Nubia at the time he was celebrating a ritual in the forecourt of the temple of Amun at Karnak, went immediately into the holy of holies to consult Amun. After this tête-à-tête with the god, he proclaimed the decisions that had been made.[12] Under similar circumstances, Hatshepsut, alone in her father's sanctuary, heard an order that came from the mouth of the god.[13]

Until the fourth century B.C.E., spoken oracles remained an exception, and both ordinary individuals and officials were informed of divine intentions and plans by the movement of the processional barque, which was interrogated with due solemnity on the occasion of a divine procession. When the deity approved, the priestly bearers of the festival barque would feel themselves overwhelmed by its weight, or they would feel the barque turning toward one of the written propositions that had been presented to the deity. Egyptians could also address a deity directly, either in silent prayer or with a written prayer that was displayed for all eternity in a temple or in the tomb of the faithful. Apart from the quality of the author and the nature of the request, the content of these individual prayers proceeded from the same theological bases as the hymns of the collective cults.

The choice of a specific image to serve as an intermediary was one of the characteristics of what is called *popular piety*. One would choose a particular spot in the decoration of a temple, such as the large image of Ptah in the passageway through the fortified gate of the temple of Medinet Habu. This image—clothed, sheltered, and even gilded—served as a point of communication between persons of humble status and the great deities of Egypt. Sometimes, the intercessor was an ancient notable whose statue bore an inscription addressed to those who visited the temple: "Tell me your prayers, that I may transmit them to the mistress of the Two Lands, for she hears my prayers."

DIVINE PRESENCE ON EARTH

Communication between the human and divine realms often took place via a manufactured object—an image or a statue animated by the Opening of the Mouth ritual. The cult was a means of causing and prolonging the localized presence of a deity. Conversely, the immanence of the forces of the universe implied a divine presence that was continuous and diffuse, yet excluded from ritual action, except in the special case of solar cults. This polarity was also true of persons: individuals could address prayers to deities wherever they were, but ritual acts—especially collective ones—always took place where divine presence was concentrated. There were, however, certain natural points of concentration of divinity.

Animals

Because animals were living beings inflicted with the inability to communicate with humans, it was easy to think that they had privileged relations with the imaginary side of the world. The Buchis bull of Hermonthis, a city a little south of Thebes, was "the living *ba* of Re, herald of Re." This unique animal, the incarnation of Re, was recognizable by certain markings. The Apis bull of Memphis was the living *ba* of Ptah, whereas the Mnevis bull was that of Re at Heliopolis. Unique, sacred animals were buried with great pomp in the presence of the king or one of his representatives. An unmarked animal of the same species belonged to the profane world, yet it remained a "possible echo of the divine." The custom of raising such animals began in Dynasty 18. Pious individuals, including pilgrims, desirous of attracting divine favor assumed the cost of embalming and burying the dead animals. A recent study has shown that the animals in the large collective cemeteries (e.g., fish, crocodiles, ibises, cats, and dogs) had been reverently strangled, drowned, or dispatched with blows from a cudgel or ax. These hecatombs were carried out on animals of all ages at a certain time of the year: during festivals, the pilgrims' demand for mummies took precedence over the natural mortality of the livestock.

A number of species living in the wild were considered manifestations of deities. The serpent Ikher was a manifestation of Re when he died and a manifestation of Kherybeqef when the numbing effect of winter weakened the strength of its venom.

THE DIVINE AND THE KING
The Concept of Maat

The king, a living symbol of humanity, touched the divine realm while remaining anchored in the real and the human. His duty was to cause Maat to reign on earth. Daughter of Re, the solar sovereign, Maat was a deified concept. She represented order—that which needed to be done so that the world would function harmoniously and thus subsist. Jan Assmann has defined Maat as the very principle of social cohesion[14]: those who acted according to Maat practiced justice, spoke the truth, acted for the good of the collectivity, and communicated and played their role in the social chain. Maat was the expression in the divine realm of the social solidarity of the pharaonic state. Texts affirm that Re nourished himself on Maat, which is to say that divinity, and thus creation, subsisted because social cohesion was respected.

As administrator of the land, the king was responsible for the functioning of the temples. He alone, as representative of humanity, was authorized to dialogue with the gods and goddesses. The mythological model of the kingship was essentially solar and Heliopolitan. In the temple of Luxor, Amenophis III is depicted as an officiant of the sun god. Pharaoh's divinity was partial: only his office and its external signs were sacred (see p. 65). As liturgical actor, he played a divine role, acting "like" the gods in the course of ritual ("Pharaoh ludens").[15] Theoretically, the mortuary offering that assured survival in the hereafter for the least of his subjects was presented by the king. But the king was also a man, and, sometimes, even a man with a dubious political past. Certain sovereigns left evidence of personal devotion similar to that of their subjects. Other evidence concerns the legitimacy of their power. In the Ptolemaic Period, the priests of the small temple at Deir el-Medina added a mammisi to their temple to celebrate the power of young Ptolemy VI Philometor, who was five years of age, and to affirm the regency of his mother Cleopatra I, the Syrian.

DEITIES AND INDIVIDUALS
Deities in the Individual Conscience

The Egyptians loved their gods and goddesses. Happy was "he who placed him in his heart" (i.e., the one who knew a god and placed him in his conscience). The authors of wisdom literature often spoke of a "god" whom it was necessary to honor and revere. This anonymous being has been interpreted as an indication of a "monotheism of the learned," but it seems that this unnamed "god" was the local deity of the potential reader (see p. 99). When the author alluded to a divine function, the deity was named: the wrath of the divine was that of Sakhmet or Hathor.

Deities were feared because they could intervene directly in the lives of individuals. A certain Huy gave false testimony and swore to it, but some days later, "divine *bau* appeared"[16]—without doubt in the form of some physical ill that befell the perjurer. Theophoric names were extremely common: Amun-is-mighty, Mut-destroys-the-evil-eye, It-is-pleasant-with-Ptah, and so forth. Tjaasetemimu (*c.* 370 B.C.E.) placed himself under the protection of the personal goddess Semset of Perdfau, an ancient protectress of the year who was recycled in the role of a guardian angel: "I have nourished you," said the goddess, "and I have made your strength grow."[17] In Demotic texts of the Late Period, we find Petbe, deity of the conscience of the individual, who punishes perjury before the gods.[18]

Gods as Recourse of a Social Group

The ties binding certain deities and certain professional categories were of two types. One type stemmed from the specific mythology of a deity: thus, Ptah, conceiver and artisan of the world, was especially honored by sculptors, carvers, and other craftsmen. Thoth, patron of scribes, also belongs in this category, along with Montu the warrior, who was popular with the Medjay—a sort of desert police; Sakhmet, the patroness of physicians and veterinarians; Selqet, the scorpion goddess who was mistress of healers; and other deities as well. The other type of bond resulted from occasional local encounters: quarrymen displayed a special devotion to Anukis, mistress of Elephantine and its quarries, or to Min, lord of the quarries of the Wadi Hammamat near his city.

Gods Diverted, Constrained, or Threatened

To force events to turn out in their favor or in that of their client, magicians did not hesitate to employ threats. The means were legitimate, because their victim was Seth: "Stop, crocodile, son of Seth! . . . may the water be a blazing flame for you." But it happened that more innocent deities were abused by magicians: the lords of Heliopolis would be burned, the cow Hathor would be decapitated, and, most horrible of all, Sobek the crocodile and Anubis the dog would be covered with the skins of a crocodile and a dog. In the Book of the Heavenly Cow, Re himself seems to fear *hekau*-magic. A passage in the Coffin Texts informs us that, as a tool of the creator, *hekau*-magic existed before anything else.

8

Geography and the Gods

CITIES AND GODS

The Deity of a City

For city dwellers and villagers alike, the most important deity was the one whose residence was nearest: "The voice of the god of the city ordains the death and the life of its people."[1] The responsibility of a deity vis-à-vis a region was independent of his or her personality. The relations between deities and humans were regulated by cultic consensus: if the rituals were carried out and the divine altars were provisioned, all would be well. But beware the consequences of the frivolity of undependable officiants!

Thus, at Dendara, if a gossipy priest revealed the appearance of the secret images of the deities in the House of Gold, or if the god found a group of people gawking in this sacrosanct place, he would be "greatly wroth against his city." If, however, the rituals were carried out as prescribed, the god would expel "every evil from his city, as well as the entire land" and bring "an abundant inundation," and "the meadows will be green."[2] (Note that the author of this inscription in the temple of Hathor uses the word *god* and not *goddess*, because of the gender neutrality of the concept of "city god.")

Citizens who respected Maat were obliged to take part in the cult of the city god: "Celebrate the festival of your god and repeat it at its time,"[3] recommended Any, the Dynasty 18 sage. The entire population would participate in the great processional rituals whose prophylactic benefits were felt by all: Hatshepsut presented a processional statue of Hathor to the temple of Cusae "so that her city might be protected by the barque of processions by land."[4] The deity's emergence from the temple—a solemn and public manifestation of divine presence in the city—was also the emergence of a sovereign making an appearance before his people. When his divine duties led him out of his temple of Karnak to traverse his city, Amun was called "prince of Thebes." The loyalty of a citizen could border on chauvinism: "I have made no city prosper except your city," declared an enthusiastic devotee.

Deities Outside Their City

To encourage visitors to his funerary chapel to recite the offering formula on his behalf, Djau (c. 2250 B.C.E.) promised them the blessings of "the god of their city," whether near or far, god or goddess. The so-called "Saite" formula, carved on the dorsal pillar of the statues of important individuals that were placed in temples, set them under the protection of their city god, although the deity remained unnamed.

A city god was not immobile. Such deities followed the peregrinations of their faithful. Egyptian gods and goddesses were omnipresent and accessible everywhere, whether by individual prayer or cult. But this fact did not prevent Egyptians from feeling a personal attachment to a cult place. In such a case, anonymity was lost, and the name of the local deity would be followed by a topographical qualification. In the enclosure of the temple of Amun at Karnak, Amenophis II constructed a chapel dedicated to "Amun of Perunefer," from the name of the royal shipyards at Memphis, the city where the young king had received his military and administrative training.

When Egyptians traveled, their attachment to their city god did not exclude consideration of the deities of other cities. The latter could be of service to them as mediators with their own city god. On a trip to the north in 1072 B.C.E., Heqanefer, the second prophet of Amun, wrote to his friend Tjaroi, an administrator in the Theban necropolis, "Each day, I pray each god and goddess before whom I pass to grant you life, prosperity, and health," along with a happy retirement "in the following of Amun of Karnak, our lord."[5]

Deities as Personifications of Cities

On returning from his eighth campaign in Syria, the valorous Tuthmosis III ordained the setting up of a statue of "Victorious Thebes" and the establishment of a cult for it. Victorious Thebes (*Waset*), image of the warlike values of the sovereigns who issued from her, had the appearance of a woman armed with a lance, a club, a bow, and arrows. Her litanies intoned the names of Egyptian cities whose mistress was Hathor or one of her bellicose forms. The goddess was She-who-is-before-her-lord (*Khefethernebes*), symbolizing both the city and the fortification that protected the divine lord of Thebes. In the reign of Sethos I, Waset had counterparts at Memphis: the goddesses Mennefer and Tjesemet. The name of the former was the name of the city; the name of the latter was derived from a word meaning "bastion." Tjesemet's headdress represented a sort of crenelated bastion, justifying the words of the sage: "The walls of a city are its gods."

DEITIES AND PROVINCES

Throughout the land, the special features of each sanctuary, along with its liturgical history and its traditions, were carefully set down on fragile rolls of papyrus in the local priestly library. In the later periods of Egyptian history, certain texts were copied onto materials impervious to worms, such as the walls of the great Greco-Roman temples. According to one of the monumental inscriptions on the pylon of the temple of Isis at Philae, its walls were "inscribed with the divine company of this nome, along with the prescriptions concerning it."[6] Here, the decoration of the walls is considered to be an inventory of the deities and cults of the region.

The little, local cults could be quite numerous. Writing to the lady Sakhmetnofret, the lady Stika of Memphis commended her Theban friend not only to Ptah, "lord of Ankhhtawy" (Memphis), but also to "every god and every goddess who is in the region of Memphis"—no fewer than thirty-three deities of every sort (e.g., Ptah-under-his-moringa, Amun-of-the-lettuce, Qadesh, and so forth), as well as the kings buried in the necropolis and the other deceased.

The Nomes

Along the bases of walls in the later temples, long lines of personages with the appearance of Nile genies face the lord of the temple, bringing him all the products of the land. Each of these personages represents a nome. The forty-two nomes were provinces representing, on average, approximately twenty-five miles along the course of the river. Prior to the fourth century B.C.E., these processions of nomes announced only the names of the provinces with no further details. In the Ptolemaic Period, under Ptolemy VIII (145–116 B.C.E.), these processions became veritable encyclopedias of religious geography covering four topics: the nome and its principal deity, its canal, its cultivable fields, and its marshes. The goal of these lists was not to describe a cultic reality—much less a political one—but to exalt the prosperity of the entire land delivering its products to the deity of the temple. Nome by nome, mythological grounds justify this delivery by establishing clever, erudite correspondences between the theology of the deity receiving the goods and that of the nome that produced them. The priests of Koptos took the game further by assigning the products of each nome to a different Koptite divine beneficiary.

These documents are succinct, allusive, and partial. Thus, the nineteenth nome of Upper Egypt and the eleventh nome of Lower Egypt were treated abusively by the compilers of the geographic processions in the great temple of Horus at Edfu, for they were home to Seth; the texts claim that the canal was dried out, the temples were in ruins, and the titles of the priests had been forgotten. At Koptos, the list of nomes on the gateway of the temple of Geb, the goodly crocodile, disdainfully omits four nomes of Horus gods who were natural enemies of this animal, including Edfu and Dendara.[7]

Early Geographic Lists

In earlier periods, the company of the deities of Egypt was loosely distributed and ignored the division into nomes. When Amenophis IV decided to establish a cult for his solar god at Karnak, he had all the deities of Egypt contribute to it and requested that the divine domains throughout the land contribute a small sum. The order of the list of ninety sanctuaries taxed by the "royal mystic" is strictly geographic, running from south to north and ignoring the order in which the nomes were usually listed. The same arrangement governs the list of city gods that runs along the interior walls of the terrace of the Temple of Millions of Years of Ramesses III at Medinet Habu.

The base of each of the criosphinxes of the western dromos at Karnak, which today number ninety-eight, bears a brief inscription placing the king under the protection of the deity of a city. This list displays nothing like the hypothetical rigor of the late lists, and it shows a decided preference for the deities nearest Thebes.

Late Compilations

To render an account of the richness of the local traditions scattered throughout the many sanctuaries—great and small—that dotted the land, scholars and ritualists of the last centuries of Egyptian history put together regional compilations that constituted a sort of report on the theological status of the locales. The most beautiful example of this type of document is Papyrus Jumilhac of the Ptolemaic Period, now in the Louvre Museum. A good thirty feet in length, this roll of papyrus collects all the local legends concerning the deities and rituals of the seventeenth and eighteenth nomes of Upper Egypt (i.e., the region of Beni Mazar in Middle Egypt). It is written in the classical language, but it has numerous Demotic turns of expression that betray the role of the author/compiler and commentator. The work is divided into three main sections: (1) deities of the region related to Anubis and regional deities related to Osiris and his myth; (2) the sacred objects, beings, and places of the region; and (3) the cult places of the god Duanwy and their legends. Various versions of a single myth or an etymology are set down side by side with a remarkable care for documentary objectivity. One scholar has proposed that the author of the papyrus was a bilingual scholar conversant with Greek literature.[8] This thesaurus of regional, religious geography was frequently consulted, as shown by the many annotations in the Demotic script found in the margins of the papyrus.

Other regions of Egypt were the object of works of the same sort. Two of these works have survived: the Book of the Faiyum, which has several known versions, and Papyrus Brooklyn 47.218.84, which is devoted to the delta. The priests of the Greco-Roman Period made an effort to impose some degree of order on the profusion of local theologies with the aid of these manuals. The Tanis Papyrus, dated to the reign of Hadrian, contains a nome-by-nome list of sacred objects. The holy of holies of the temple of Edfu displays a series of monographs, nome by nome, detailing deities, cults, clergies and their titles, sacred barques, festivals, taboos, tutelary genies, and so forth.

DEITIES OF THE MARCHES AND FRONTIERS
The Gateways to the Desert

Omnipresent in the Egyptian landscape, the desert was itself foreign territory. The presence of the departure point of a desert trail made a province of the valley into a march whose deities could be taken out of the valley and into the desert. Min of Koptos, the ithyphallic god of the fifth nome of Upper Egypt, was thus the guardian of the rich mining areas of the eastern desert to which his city commanded the access. He protected the quarrymen and prospectors who traversed the eastern desert. He was "lord of life," assuring the survival of work crews in the heart of the desert. From the New Kingdom on, Amun enjoyed a cult in el-Kharga Oasis, which was accessible from the region of Thebes.

To these migrant gods, who were borne by the faithful, were added deities specific to the desert environment, such as Seth. Around 900 B.C.E., Seth had an oracular temple at Mut, the capital of el-Dakhla Oasis, and his presence is well-attested at el-Kharga Oasis. Hathor frequented these places from the Middle Kingdom on. Devastating in her leonine form of Sakhmet prowling in the desert, she was mistress of joy and love when she returned, appeased, to the valley. As sovereign of the desert areas, Hathor was "mistress of turquoise"—the precious mineral extracted from the distant mines of the Sinai.

The Mercenaries of the Delta Marches

When the marches gave access to zones that were frequented by populations of another culture, the divine realm was peopled by hybrid personages; we are not always sure whether we are dealing with former Egyptian deities more or less disguised as foreigners to assure domination of the marches or with foreign deities who had become Egyptianized. Sometimes, the divine combatant's regular contact with his hereditary local enemy ended by contaminating him. Thus, on the western fringe of the delta, the very ancient god Ash, known from Dynasty 3, became "lord of the Libyans" in the New Kingdom; subsequently, he assumed the visage of Seth, and in later periods of history, he became a divine enemy.

The most important of these deities was Sopd, the Horian god of Saft el-Hinna, Egypt's gateway to the eastern confines of the delta. The earliest representations of Sopd, dating to Dynasty 5, show him curiously decked out in a beard of Asiatic style. Was Sopd, as Jean Yoyotte has put it, "a naturalized Egyptian soldier, or an Egyptian officer dressed up in native guise"?[9] Sopd, whose name means "the bearded one," was a bellicose being who "trampled the Asiatics." As "lord of the east," he symbolized the east, and his counterparts were Rahes (the west), Dedwen (the south), and Horus (the north). From these givens, the learned scribes at Saft el-Hinna in the fourth century B.C.E. developed a complex theology in which the former native god took on the functions of Shu.

Deities as Guests in Nubia

The situation was rather different in the southern marches. Nubia—the source of valuable products such as gold, ebony, ivory, and incense—was the southern extension of Egypt. At various times, Egyptian sovereigns attempted to assimilate and Egyptianize this relatively unpopulated and remote area.

The god Dedwen, "lord of Nubia," had a non-Egyptian name. Though he is often cited in texts as god of the south and purveyor of incense, Dedwen had no cult place in Egypt. He was, however, worshiped in Nubia from the Middle Kingdom on. Several purely Egyptian deities were introduced into Nubia for functional reasons, such as Min, protector of those who searched for gold at Quban and Buhen, and Wepwawet, "opener of the ways" and god of Asyut and Quban. Khnum of Elephantine and his consorts Satis and Anukis were present as deities of the river and its cataracts. The Nubian Hathor was a form of the Distant Goddess. It was Thoth, lord of Pnubs, who was able to bring this goddess back; he was assisted by Bes, who by this act became "lord of Punt," because this bearded gnome was not a god of Nubian origin. The temple of Thoth at el-Dakka, built under Ptolemy II, was the Lower Nubian substitute for his actual sanctuary at Pnubs, located nearly 200 miles to the south.

We know little about the Horus gods of Nubia: Horus of Miam (Aniba), of Baki (Quban), of Buhen, and of Meha (known from Dynasty 18) were connected, perhaps, with the royal ideology. The cult of the deified king is attested in Nubia from the Middle Kingdom (cult of Senwosret III at Semna). It expanded in the New Kingdom with the jubilee temples of Amenophis III and Teye at Soleb and Sedeinga and the speoi of Ramesses II.

Amun occupied a preponderant place in the Nubian cults in the Middle Kingdom (Quban) and under Dynasty 18 (Amada, Kawa, and Soleb). Much later, the sovereigns of Dynasty 25 and their successors from Upper Nubia would lay claim to Amun of Gebel Barkal in the region of Napata.

In the Greco-Roman Period, several edifices would be dedicated to the cult of Isis and Osiris at Dabod, Tafa, Kalabsha, and el-Maharraqa.

Nubian Deities

Nubian deities with Egyptianized names made their appearance during the Greco-Roman Period. Mandulis, god of Talmis (Kalabsha), was a child god and a solar son god who appeared in the double form of Mandulis the Child and the Elder Mandulis, the two falcons decorated with flowers. Arensnuphis, "goodly arrival," was the Egyptian interpretation of a Nubian name. Worshiped at Philae, he was assimilated to Shu in the role of the one who recovered the Distant Goddess. Finally, in the region of the Sixth Cataract, the sovereigns of Meroe, who were contemporaries of the Ptolemies, built temples of Pharaonic inspiration at Musawwarat el-Sufra and Naqa; there, Amun, Shu, and Tefnut were to be found side by side with two warrior deities who were sometimes represented with lions' heads, Apademak and Sebiumeker. At Naqa, Apademak—or Pairmek, "the protector," with a false Egyptian etymology—was depicted as an Indian deity endowed with three heads and four arms.

DEITIES FROM OTHER PLACES

During the New Kingdom, certain deities from the east slipped into the divine realm of Egypt. Although these gods and goddesses were the products of non-Egyptian thought, they were entirely *netjeru* "gods."

The treaty concluded by Ramesses III and Hattusilis III was guaranteed by the "thousand male and female deities of the land of Hatti and the thousand male and female deities of the land of Egypt." In the list that follows, the numerous storm gods of this or that city are considered as many local forms of the Egyptian god Seth, freeing the Egyptians from having to draw up cumbersome concordances between the two pantheons.

The presence of approximately ten foreign deities in Egypt was not solely the result of a social group of foreign origin. The warrior kings of Dynasty 18, in particular Amenophis II, were attached to these gods and goddesses, and they vaunted their warlike values in terms of foreign belief systems.

Reshep seems to have been one of the personal tutelary deities of Amenophis II. This warrior god connected to horses and cavalry is mentioned in the king's chapel at Karnak. From the same reign stems the first attestation, at Perunefer, of Astarte, the goddess of warfare and horses, who is sometimes depicted nude. Anat, "mistress of the gods of the king" and "mother" of Ramesses II, was introduced into Egypt during this king's reign. The goddesses Anat and Astarte and the god Reshep wear the same unisex outfit: a tight-fitting gown and a tall headdress similar to the white crown and decorated with a gazelle's head like a sort of uraeus. All three deities gesticulate in a manner that is scarcely Egyptian and brandish a club and a shield. Reshep and Astarte were still being mentioned in the Ptolemaic Period.

Baal, who was present in the onomasticon over a long period of time, was assimilated to Seth. He was first mentioned as a god in the reign of Amenophis II. Around the time of Dynasty 25, his cult suffered the consequences of the demonization of Seth.

The Great Sphinx of Giza was identified with Haurun, a Canaanite falcon god, from the reign of Tuthmosis III on. He was regarded as one of the personal tutelary deities of Ramesses II.

These deities always bore signs of their foreign origin, whether in the iconography or in their titles (e.g., Haurun of the Lebanon, Astarte of Syria). They were sometimes endowed with an Egyptian parentage: Reshep was son of Harsaphes of Herakleopolis, Astarte was the daughter of Ptah, and Anat was the daughter of Re. But these were functional designations stressing the violent, Horian aspect of the gods and the dangerous, Hathoric charms of the goddesses.

We have two mythological accounts depicting these deities. One of them, a story, is unfortunately quite fragmentary.[10] The brutal and greedy Payom, god of the sea, terrorizes and makes demands of the deities of Egypt. In their distress, they send Astarte to him—without success, it seems. Finally, they appeal to the belligerent god Seth. The safety of the fertile land hangs on the colossal battle between the untamed forces of the terrestrial desert and the furious elements of the liquid desert. This original work is an exotic and picturesque transposition of the combat of Seth and Apopis. It draws its inspiration from a Ugaritic mythological poem recounting the battle between Yamm, god of the sea, and Baal.

The second account is part of a magical incantation. Strolling on the beach, Seth surprises the goddess Metut as she bathes. Disconcerted by the sight of the goddess's nudity and by "the belt above her buttocks," he assaults her "in the manner of a bull" or a ram. This brutal act brings him nothing but trouble. His sperm rises to his head, and he falls ill. Like a fury, his companion Anat rushes to her father Re to solicit a cure for Seth. (Seth's indulgent accomplice Anat was a highly ambiguous figure who wore both male and female clothing; like Nephthys, Seth's Egyptian companion, she was a sterile warrior-goddess.) Happily, Isis, the fertile wife, brings things back to normal, at the same time curing the sick person who has recourse to this formula. For purely Egyptian ends, the text makes use of the violent and sensual figures of foreign goddesses and the equivocal attraction of the exotic.

The goddess Qadesh had a special place in this pantheon. She was usually represented nude, viewed full front with arms extended, and clenching lotuses or serpents in her fists (Figure 24). Sometimes, she stands on a striding lion. Not to be found in documents of royal origin, Qadesh was a goddess of the common people whose popularity seems to have been confined to the Ramesside Period. She is unknown from the pantheons of western Asia. Her name, which means "holy" in Semitic, was also that of the city on the banks of the Orontes that was the key to northern Syria. Was this Qadesh, stripped of her clothing, a goddess dreamed up by Egyptian soldiers stationed in the colonies? Whatever the case, she was provided with acolytes—either Reshep and Baal—or, more often, Reshep and the ithyphallic Min. The choice of Min indicates the erotic energy of Qadesh.

At Thebes, terra cotta models of beds have been found decorated on one surface with an image of the nude Qadesh standing in a boat. These objects, which were discovered in the rubble of ancient houses, combine the exoticism and sensuality of the nude Qadesh with the purely Egyptian decor of a garden in the style of a marsh—a pleasure spot dedicated to fecundity.[11]

EGYPTIAN DEITIES OUTSIDE EGYPT
Divine Accomplices of Colonial Rule

Egyptian hegemony found expression in rock-cut stelae and in stelae set up in the courtyards of the temples of local gods and goddesses. The deities represented on these stelae are Egyptian; they bear witness to the warlike

Geography and the Gods 109

Figure 24. The goddess Qadesh.

values of the king and receive the tribute of Asiatic cities, as on the rock-cut stelae of Ramesses II at Nahr el-Kelb near Beirut. It is uncertain whether permanent cult places were established in cities that recognized Egyptian sovereignty. Amun might have had a temple at Gaza beginning in Dynasty 18; Gaza was a frontier town that was part of the royal domain. In the land of Djahy (Palestine), Ramesses III had a chapel built that was dedicated to a statue of "Amun of Ramesses, prince of Heliopolis." The basic function of this sanctuary was to collect local products: "The Asiatics of the land of Retjenu come to him bearing their products before his holy face."[12] More than just a cult place, the chapel seems to have been an administrative and fiscal establishment, similar to the *bekhenu*-castles built by the same king in Egypt, Nubia, and Syria. Here, deities were involved in a system of economic exploitation of tributary regions.

Exported Deities

Egyptian deities were not much exported prior to the Hellenistic Period. There are Egyptian objects mentioning deities scattered through the Mediterranean world, but they are relatively rare. Calcite wine jars bearing inscriptions dating to Dynasty 22 have been found in Spain. Magnificent vases of Dynasty 6 were part of the treasure of the kings of Ebla in Syria.

Ivory plaques from luxurious items of furniture, probably beds decorated with Egyptian themes, have been discovered in the palaces of the princes of Syria-Palestine. These objects, which were locally manufactured, were inspired by motifs from Egyptian religion: the god kneeling on his lotus and protected by two winged goddesses is copied directly from the traditional decoration of portable shrines, and it reflects the effect of the splendor of Egyptian religion on the Asiatics. "Hathor of Byblos" was probably the Egyptian interpretation of a local goddess; the temple of Hathor—built there by the overseer of works, Minmes, under Tuthmosis III—was probably just a simple chapel placed in the goddess's temple. In the Hellenistic era, the cult of Tammuz of Byblos was connected with the Osirian cycle.

Egyptian deities sometimes traveled in Asia in the form of a statue endowed with special qualities. A story from the Third Intermediate Period relates the adventures of an image of Khonsu "Pa-ir-sekheru"—an oracular, healing form of the Theban god, which was sent to a legendary land to combat an evil local genie who had possessed a beautiful princess.[13] This practice of lending an efficacious image was frequent in the ancient Near East. We know that Tushratta, king of Mitanni, sent a healing statue of Astarte to Amenophis III shortly before the latter's death.

Conclusion

The world of the gods of Egypt belonged to a religion of learning that, through the millennia, accumulated knowledge of the true that justified the appearances of the real. This learned thought does not fit easily into analytical structures based on the polytheism/monotheism opposition peculiar to the prophetic religions. In Egypt, the unique being of the "first moment" contained, in potential, all the components of the true of the imaginary realm, as well as components of the givens of the real world. The multiplicity of deities was merely a development from the divine monad after the differentiation of the elements of the cosmos. Thus, if it is necessary to propose an analytical structure for the Egyptian imaginary, I would not speak of an opposition, but rather of a polarity of *indeterminate/determined*, or more practically, of *unnamed/named*. Let us take an example: the brute forces that uselessly set the desert ablaze at the margins of the civilized world, striking blindly and indiscriminately, were united in the anonymous Distant Goddess, the Powerful One (Sakhmet). Coming into contact with the Nile valley, she was appeased and tamed, at that point fueling the cycles of local theologies (e.g., the return of the inundation, the rebirth of the moon and of Osiris, the birth of the divine child, and so forth) and taking on various names: according to the cult place, the anonymous destructive goddess became Nekhbet, Isis, Anukis, Meret, and so forth.

The dichotomy of *person/function*, key to the divine combinatory, fits into the system of *unnamed/named*. The anonymous god of the wisdom texts served as the personal god of the social individual, and each person who read these texts would assign a name to him and identify him with a single deity in his environment, whether in the real (a deity housed, provided with a temple) or the imaginary. A myth, or more precisely, the divine "*ana*," was more a group of functional metaphors than the narration of the epic of a divine personage. The culmination of this system was, in the later periods of Egyptian history, the appearance of anonymous deities such as the Great Goddess of the Koptite nome or, perhaps, the Great Bull of el-Madamud—personages who combined in themselves all the functions of a category of divine beings.

There was also the individual, who had an insatiable curiosity and a feeling of powerlessness before the immensity of the imaginary. Ongoing research into the cause of the original act of differentiation led thinkers of the New Kingdom to imagine a distant, unknown, divine, and creative power who was represented with various cultic and political nuances. This difficult inquiry was pursued through the ages. In the tumultuous cosmogony of Edfu, a mysterious *ba*-bird, come from no one knew where, attributed creation to Horus: "One heard his voice, but one did not see him."

So as not to lose themselves in the immense potential of the imaginary, theologians set themselves rules that channeled and fertilized their thought. The riskier the rule, the more the coherence that they succeeded in elaborating with their erudition would seem to them to stem from the divine order. On the temple walls, there blossomed the magnificent artificial flowers of the stony theologies, for the concept of their decoration was a creative game and a means of investigating the divine realm. Hymns united divine qualities with assonances based on chapter numbers. Thus, the gods continued to watch over Egypt, and when other systems of thought came to dominate the world, some of the deities would quietly pursue their careers under various guises. Who today knows that the holy Mary the Egyptian of the church of Saint-Genès of Flavigny is none other than an avatar of the goodly, nurturing Renenutet-Thermuthis?

Notes

I

The Sources and the State of Our Knowledge

1. On the mortuary literature discussed in this section, see E. Hornung, *The Ancient Egyptian Books of the Afterlife* (Ithaca, N.Y., 1999).
2. See E. Otto, *Das ägyptische Mundöffnungsritual*. 2 vols. Ägyptologische Abhandlungen 3 (Wiesbaden, 1960). The English-language edition by E. A. W. Budge, *The Book of Opening the Mouth: The Egyptian Texts with English Translations*, Books on Egypt and Chaldea 26–27 (London, 1909), is dated and thus somewhat less reliable. For a discussion of the ritual, see D. Lorton, "The Theology of Cult Statues in Ancient Egypt," in M. B. Dick (ed.), *Born in Heaven, Made on Earth: The Making of the Cult Image in the Ancient Near East* (Winona Lake, Ind., 1999), pp. 147–179.
3. The standard edition remains that of A. Moret, *Le Rituel du culte divin journalier en Égypte d'après les papyrus de Berlin et les textes du temple de Séti Ier à Abydos* (Paris, 1902; reprint ed. Geneva, 1988). The ritual has been discussed by Lorton, "The Theology of Cult Statues," pp. 131–145.
4. The papyrus has been translated by R. O. Faulkner, *Journal of Egyptian Archaeology* 22–24 (1936–1938).
5. M. Bellion, *Catalogue des manuscrits hiéroglyphiques et hiératiques publiés et signalés* (Paris, 1987), pp. 20–203; E. Devéria, *Catalogue des manuscrits égyptiens* (Paris, 1972), p. 93; J.-C. Goyon, *Kêmi* 19 (1969): 23–65.
6. H. W. Fairman, *The Triumph of Horus: An Ancient Egyptian Sacred Drama* (Berkeley, 1974).

7. The New Kingdom versions have been edited by Hellmut Brunner, *Die Geburt des Gottkönigs: Studien zur Überlieferung eines altägyptischen Mythos*, Ägyptologische Abhandlungen 10 (Wiesbaden, 1964).
8. See A. H. Gardiner, *Zeitschrift für aegyptische Sprache und Altertumskunde* 42 (1905): 12–42. Selections from the papyrus are translated by J. A. Wilson in J. B. Pritchard (ed.), *Ancient Near Eastern Texts Relating to the Old Testament*, 2d ed. (Princeton 1955), pp. 8 and 368–369.
9. For a translation of the hymn, see Wilson in Pritchard (ed.), *Ancient Near Eastern Texts*, pp. 364–367.
10. For an English translation, see M. Lichtheim, *Ancient Egyptian Literature: A Book of Readings*, vol. 1: *The Old and Middle Kingdoms* (Berkeley, 1973), pp. 204–210.
11. The edition usually consulted is that of N. de G. Davies, *The Rock Tombs of El Amarna*, Egypt Exploration Society Archaeological Survey of Egypt 13–18 (London, 1903–1908), whose translations are somewhat dated. A fresh translation of the texts has been made by W. J. Murnane, *Texts from the Amarna Period in Egypt*, Writings from the Ancient World 5 (Atlanta, 1995).
12. For a translation, see Lichtheim, *Ancient Egyptian Literature*, vol. 2: *The New Kingdom* (Berkeley, 1976), pp. 203–211.
13. For the Contendings of Horus and Seth, see Ibid., pp. 214–223. For a translation of the Legend of the God of the Sea, see Wilson in Pritchard (ed.), *Ancient Near Eastern Texts*, pp. 17–18.
14. For an English translation, see A. Piankoff, *The Shrines of Tut-Ankh-Amon*, Bollingen Series 40/2 (New York, 1955), pp. 27–34.
15. J. Assmann, *Ägyptische Hymnen und Gebete* (Zurich, 1975).
16. On the Houses of Life and temple libraries, see A. H. Gardiner, "The House of Life," *Journal of Egyptian Archaeology* 24 (1938): 157–179; P. Derchain, *Le Papyrus Salt 825 (B. M. 10051): Rituel pour la conservation de la vie en Égypte*, 2 vols., Koninklijke Academie van België, Verhandelingen 58 (Brussels, 1965); G. Burkard, "Bibliotheken im Alten Ägypten," *Bibliothek* 4 (1980): 79–115 and S. Schott, *Bücher und Bibliotheken im Alten Ägypten: Verzeichnis der Buch- und Spruchtitel und der Termini Technici*, ed. E. Schott (Wiesbaden, 1990).
17. H. Beinlich, *Das Buch vom Fayum: Zum Religiösen eigenverständnis einer ägyptischen Landschaft*, Ägyptologische Abhandlungen 51 (Wiesbaden, 1991).
18. Papyrus Brooklyn 47.218.84; see S. Sauneron, *The Brooklyn Museum Annual* 8 (1967): 99–100 and *The Brooklyn Museum Annual* 10 (1969): 110.
19. See J. Vandier, *Le Papyrus Jumilhac* (Paris, 1962).
20. See N. de G. Davies, *The Temple of Hibis in el-Khargheh Oasis*, vol. 3, pls. 2–5. The texts accompanying the representations are translated by E. Cruz-Uribe, *Hibis Temple Project*, vol. 1: *Translations, Commentary, Discussions and Sign List* (San Antonio, 1988), pp. 1–43.

21. On Greek traditions of visits to Egypt by famous men of the past, see S. Sauneron, *The Priests of Ancient Egypt* (Ithaca, N.Y., 2000), pp. 110–115.
22. A. Deiber, *Clément d'Alexandrie et l'Égypte*, Mémoires de l'Institut Français d'Archéologie 10 (Cairo, 1904). Clement is cited by J.-F. Champollion, *Le Panthéon égyptien* (Paris, 1823), s.v. "Le Bélier."
23. *Deorum concilium*, 10–11.
24. Benoît de Maillet, *Description de l'Égypte, composée sur les mémoires de M. de Maillet, ancien consul de France au Caire par M. l'Abbé Le Mascrier* (Paris, 1735).
25. *Description de l'Égypte, ou recueil des observation et des recherches qui ont été faites en Égypte pendant l'expédition de l'armée française, publié par les ordres de sa Majesté l'Empereur Napoléon le Grand*, 23 vols. (Paris, 1809–1822). For an edition of the plates with commentaries in English, see C. C. Gillispie and M. Dewachter, *Monuments of Egypt: The Napoleonic Edition* (Princeton, 1987). For a study of Egyptian religion as seen by the authors of the *Description*, see C. Traunecker, "Visions utopistes et réalité archéologique dans l'ancienne Égypte de la *Description*," in *L'Expédition d'Égypte: Une entreprise des lumières, 1798–1801* (Paris, 1999), pp. 187–203. See also C. Traunecker, "L'Égypte antique de la *Description*," in H. Laurens et al., *L'Expédition d'Égypte 1798–1801* (Paris, 1989), pp. 351–370.
26. J.-F. Champollion, *Lettres écrites d'Égypte et de Nubie en 1828 et 1829* (Paris, 1938), letter of February 10, 1829; idem, *Le Panthéon égyptien* (Paris, 1823), s.v. "Le Bélier."
27. P. Le Page Renouf, *The Origin and Growth of Religion as Illustrated by the Religion of Ancient Egypt* (New York, 1880).
28. H. K. Brugsch, *Religion und Mythologie der alten Aegypter*, 2d ed. (Leipzig, 1891; reprinted, Leipzig, 1969).
29. G. Maspero, *Études de mythologie et d'archéologie égyptiennes*, 8 vols., Bibliothèque Égyptologique 1–2, 7–8, 27–29, 40 (Paris, 1893–1913).
30. P. Pierret, *Essai sur la Mythologie Égyptienne* (1879).
31. V. Loret, *L'Égypte au temps du totémisme: Conférence faite au Musée Guimet le 9 avril 1905* (Paris, 1906).
32. E. Amélineau, *Prolégomènes à l'Étude de la Religion Égyptienne: Essai sur la mythologie de l'Égypte*, 2 vols. (Paris, 1908–1916).
33. P. Virey, *La Religion de l'ancienne Égypte*, Études sur l'Histoire des Religions 4 (Paris, 1910).
34. A. van Gennep, *Religions, moeurs et légendes: Essai d'ethnographie et de linguistique* (Paris, 1908).
35. G. Foucart, *La Méthode comparative dans l'histoire des religions* (Paris, 1909).
36. E. Meyer, *Geschichte des Alten Aegyptens* (Berlin, 1887 and many subsequent editions); *Aegypten zur Zeit der Pyramidenerbauer*, 2d ed. (Leipzig, 1908).
37. K. Wiedemann, "God (Egyptian)," in J. Hastings (ed.), *Encyclopedia of Religion and Ethics* (Edinburgh, 1913), pp. 275–277.

38. K. Sethe, *Urgeschichte und älteste Religion der Ägypter* (Leipzig, 1930).
39. H. Kees, *Der Götterglaube im Alten Aegypten* (Leipzig, 1941).
40. G. A. Wainwright, *The Sky Religion in Egypt: Its Antiquity & Effects*, (Cambridge, 1938).
41. E. J. Baumgartel, *The Cultures of Prehistoric Egypt* (London, 1947).
42. H. Junker, *Die Götterlehre von Memphis (Schabaka-Inschrift)*, Abhandlungen der Preussischen Akademie der Wissenschaften, Philosophisch-historische Klasse, Jahrgang 1939, no. 23 (Berlin, 1940).
43. E. Drioton, *La Religion égyptienne dans ses grandes lignes* (Cairo, 1945).
44. J. Sainte Fare Garnot, *La Vie religieuse dans l'ancienne Égypte* (Paris, 1948).
45. J. Vandier, *La Religion égyptienne: Précédée d'une introduction à l'histoire des religions* "Mana," Introduction à l'histoire des religions 1, Les anciennes religions orientales 1, 3d ed. (Paris, 1949).
46. C. Desroches-Noblecourt, *Ancient Egypt: The New Kingdom and the Amarna Period* (Greenwich, Conn., 1960).
47. F. Daumas, *Les Dieux de l'Égypte*, "Que sais-je?" 1194 (Paris, 1965).
48. H. Frankfort and H. A. Frankfort, in H. Frankfort et al., *The Intellectual Adventure of Ancient Man* (Chicago, 1946), pp. 11–36.
49. P. Derchain, "La Religion égyptienne," in H.-C. Puech (ed.), *Histoire des religions*, vol. 2, *La Formation des religions universelles et les religions de salut dans le monde méditerranéen et le Proche-Orient: Les Religions constituées en occident et leurs contre-courants*, Encyclopédie de la Pléiade, vol. 34 (Paris, 1970), pp. 63–140; articles "Anthropologie," "Cosmogonie," "Divinité," and "Rituels égyptiens," in P. Poupard (ed.), *Dictionnaire des Religions* (Paris, 1984).
50. S. Sauneron, *Les Prêtres de l'ancienne Égypte*, 2d ed. (Paris, 1998), translated into English by D. Lorton under the title *The Priests of Ancient Egypt* (Ithaca, N.Y., 2000); S. Sauneron and J. Yoyotte, "La Naissance du monde selon l'Égypte ancienne," in *La Naissance du monde: Égypte ancienne, Sumer, Akkad, Hourrites et Hittites, Canaan, Israel, Islam, Turcs et Mongols, Iran préislamique, Inde, Siam, Laos, Tibet, Chine*, Sources Orientales 1 (Paris, 1959).
51. E. Hornung, *Der Eine und die Vielen: Ägyptische Gottesvorstellungen* (Darmstadt, 1971), translated into English by J. Baines with the title *Conceptions of God in Ancient Egypt: The One and the Many* (Ithaca, N.Y., 1982).
52. See, for instance, the synthesis of his views in J. Assmann, *Ägypten: Theologie und Frömmigkeit einer frühen Hochkultur*, 2d ed. (Stuttgart, 1991), translated into English by D. Lorton with the title *The Search for God in Ancient Egypt* (Ithaca, N.Y., 2001).
53. P. Derchain, *Le Papyrus Salt 825: Rituel pour la conservation de la vie en Égypte*, Académie Royale de Belgique, Classe des Lettres et des Sciences Morales et Politiques, Mémoires, 2. sér., 58 (Brussels, 1965).

2
The World of the Ancient Egyptians

1. A. de Sélincourt, *Herodotus: The Histories* (Harmondsworth, 1954), p. 136 (= *Histories*, bk. 2, chap. 18).
2. Spell 571: De Buck, *The Egyptian Coffin Texts*, vol. 6, Oriental Institute Publications 81 (Chicago, 1956), p. 171. For translations, see R. O. Faulkner, *The Ancient Egyptian Coffin Texts*, vol. 2 (Warminster, 1976), p. 172; P. Barguet, *Texctes des Sarcophages égyptiens du Moyen Empire* (Paris, 1986), p. 598.
3. J. Assmann, *Ma'at: L'Égypte pharaonique et l'idée de justice sociale* (Paris, 1989) and *Ma'at: Gerechtigkeit und Unsterblichkeit im Alten Ägypten*, 2d ed. (Munich, 1995).
4. M. Lichtheim, *Ancient Egyptian Literature: A Book of Readings*, vol. 1: *The Old and Middle Kingdoms* (Berkeley, 1973), p. 206.
5. G. Daressy, "Une Inondation à Thèbes sous le règne d'Osorkon II," in *Receuil de Travaux Relatifs à la Philologie et à l'Archéologie Égyptiennes et Assyriennes* 18 (1896).
6. The text has been published by C. Vandersleyen, "Une Tempête sous le règne d'Amosis," *Revue d'Égyptologie* 19 (1967): 123–159. For an English translation, see E. N. Davis, "A Storm in Egypt During the Reign of Ahmose," in D. A. Hardy, *Thera and the Aegean World*, vol. 3 (London, 1990), pp. 232–235.
7. Lichtheim, *Ancient Egyptian Literature*, vol. 1, p. 141.
8. Papyrus Turin 1993: W. Pleyte and F. Rossi, *Papyrus de Turin* (Leiden, 1869–1876), pl. 131, line 13. For translations, see J. F. Borghouts, *Ancient Egyptian Magical Texts* (Leiden, 1978), p. 51; F. Lexa, *La Magie dans l'Égypte antique* (Paris, 1925), p. 45; J. A. Wilson, *Ancient Near Eastern Texts Relating to the Old Testament*, 2d ed. (Princeton, 1955), p. 12.
9. Instruction for Merikare; Lichtheim, *Ancient Egyptian Literature*, vol. 1, p. 106.
10. The principal study of the shadow is B. George, *Zu den altägyptischen Vorstellungen vom Schatten als Seele* (Bonn, 1970).
11. On the heart, see especially A. Piankoff, *Le "Coeur" dans les textes égyptiens depuis l'Ancien jusqu'à la fin du Nouvel Empire* (Paris, 1930).
12. Book of the Dead, chap. 30B; see M. Lichtheim, *Ancient Egyptian Literature: A Book of Readings*, vol. 2: *The New Kingdom* (Berkeley, 1976), p. 121.
13. G. Lefebvre, *Le Tombeau de Petosiris*, vol. 2 (Cairo, 1923), pp. 53–60 (text no. 81, line 5,); see also p. 117 (text no. 57), p. 152 (text no. 85, line 8), and p. 191 (text no. 125).
14. The principal monographs on the *ka* are L. Greven, *Der Ka in Theologie und Königskult der Ägypter des Alten Reiches*, Ägyptologische Forschungen 17 (Glückstadt, 1952) and U. Schweitzer, *Das Wesen des Ka im Diesseits und Jenseits der alten Ägypter*, Ägyptologische Forschungen 19 (Glückstadt, 1956).

15. Book of the Dead, chap. 30B. Cf. the translation of M. Lichtheim, *Ancient Egyptian Literature*, vol. 2, p. 121.
16. See J. Sainte Fare Garnot, *Aspect de l'Égypte ancienne* (Cairo, 1959), pp. 101–107.
17. See L. V. Žabkar, *A Study of the Ba Concept in Ancient Egyptian Texts*, Studies in Ancient Oriental Civilizations 34 (Chicago, 1968), pp. 162–163.
18. S. Sauneron, *Revue d'Égyptologie* 15 (1963): 49–51; see also E. Hornung, *Conceptions of God in Ancient Egypt: The One and the Many* (Ithaca, N.Y., 1982), pp. 60–62; and Sainte Fare Garnot, *Aspect de l'Égypte ancienne*, p. 111.
19. J. de Morgan, *Kom Ombo*, vol. 2 (1895), text no. 635; see A. Gutbub, *Textes fondamentaux de la théologie de Kom Ombo* (Cairo, 1973), p. 288.
20. The principal study of the *akh* is G. Englund, *Akh—Une Notion religieuse dans l'Égypte pharaonique*, Boreas, Uppsala Studies in Ancient Mediterranean and Near Eastern Civilizations 11 (Uppsala, 1978); the meaning of the root is discussed in the Introduction.
21. E. Hornung, *Les Dieux de l'Égypte* (Paris, 1986), p. 52.
22. See Y. Koenig, "Un Revenant inconvenant," dans *Bulletin de l'Institut Français d'Archéologie Orientale au Caire* 79 (1979): 105–106.
23. See especially R. J. Demarée, *The 'ḫ iḳr n R'-Stelae: On Ancestor Worship in Ancient Egypt* (Leiden, 1983).

3
The Gods and Their Universe

1. V. Loret, "Les Enseignes militaires des tribus et les symboles hiéroglyphiques des divinités," *Revue Égyptienne* 10 (1902); "L'Égypte au temps du totémisme," *Conférences du Musée Guimet* 19 (1906): 121–152; "Quelques idées sur la forme primitive de certaines religions égyptiennes," *Revue Égyptologique* 10 (1904): 69–100.
2. E. Amélineau, *Prolégomènes à l'étude de la religion égyptienne: Essai sur la mythologie de l'Égypte*, 2 vols. (Paris, 1908–1916).
3. P. Virey, *La Religion de l'ancienne Égypte*, Études sur l'Histoire des Religions 4 (Paris, 1910).
4. K. Sethe, *Urgeschichte und älteste Religion der Ägypter*, Abhandlungen für die Kunde des Morgenlandes 18/4 (Leipzig, 1930; reprinted, Nendeln, 1966).
5. G. Jéquier, *Considérations sur les religions Égyptiennes* (Neufchatel, 1946).
6. H. Kees, *Der Götterglaube im alten Aegypten*, Mitteilungen der Vorderasiatisch-Aegyptischen Gesellschaft 45 (Leipzig, 1941).
7. H. Frankfort, *Kingship and the Gods: A Study of Ancient Near Eastern Religion as the Integration of Society and Nature* (Chicago, 1948).

8. S. Morenz, *Ägyptische Religion*, Die Religionen der Menschheit 8 (Stuttgart, 1960). Translated into English by Ann E. Keep under the title *Egyptian Religion* (Ithaca, N.Y., 1973).
9. Frankfort, *Kingship and the Gods*, pp. 33–34.
10. B. G. Trigger, "The Rise of Egyptian Civilization," in B. G. Trigger et al., *Ancient Egypt: A Social History* (Cambridge, 1983), pp. 48–49.
11. Ibid., p. 46.
12. J. R. Baines, "Trône et dieu: Aspects du symbolisme royal et divin des temps archaïques," *Bulletin de la Société Française d'Égyptologie* 118 (1990): 5–37.
13. E. Hornung, *Conceptions of God in Ancient Egypt: The One and the Many*, trans. J. Baines (Ithaca, N.Y., 1971), pp. 105–107.
14. J.-F. Champollion, *Dictionnaire égyptien* (Paris, 1841), p. 345.
15. Sethe, *Urgeschichte und älteste Religion*, § 10.
16. Jéquier, *Considérations sur les religions égyptiennes*.
17. Baines, "Trône et dieu," pp. 27–31.
18. Hornung, *Conceptions of God*, p. 38.
19. D. Meeks, "Notion de 'dieu' et structure du panthéon dans l'Égypte ancienne," *Revue de l'Histoire des Religions* 205/1 (1988): 425–446.
20. See J. K. Hoffmeier, *Sacred in the Vocabulary of Ancient Egypt: The Term DSR, with Special Reference to Dynasties I–XX*, Orbis Biblicus et Orientalis 59 (Freiburg and Göttingen, 1985).
21. Papyrus Jumilhac VI, 15–16; see J. Vandier, *Le Papyrus Jumilhac* (Paris, 1961), pp. 117, 157, and 103.
22. Magical papyrus Boulaq 6, VII.1–2.
23. Ramesses IV, stela from Abydos; see K. A. Kitchen, *Ramesside Inscriptions: Historical and Biographical*, vol. 6, p. 23, line 13.
24. For a translation of the text, see J. A. Wilson in J. B. Pritchard (ed.), *Ancient Near Eastern Texts Relating to the Old Testament*, 2d ed. (Princeton, 1955), pp. 12–14.
25. Papyrus Boulaq 6.
26. Papyrus Boulaq 17; see Wilson, in *Ancient Near Eastern Texts*, p. 367.
27. Wilson, in *Ancient Near Eastern Texts*, p. 13.
28. Hymn of the king to Anukis, temple of Komir.
29. Book of the Heavenly Cow, end of Dynasty 18; see E. Hornung, *Der ägyptische Mythos von der Himmelskuh: Eine Ätiologie des Unvollkommenen*, Orbis Biblicus et Orientalis 46 (Freiburg and Göttingen, 1982), p. 47.
30. Spell 261; see R. O. Faulkner, *The Ancient Egyptian Coffin Texts*, vol. 1 (Warminster, 1973), pp. 199–201.
31. Piankhy (Piye) Stela; cf. the translation of M. Lichtheim, *Ancient Egyptian Literature: A Book of Readings*, vol. 3: *The Late Period* (Berkeley, 1980), p. 73.

32. Papyrus Leiden I 350, III.11; the text has been translated into English by A. H. Gardiner, *Zeitschrift für ägyptische Sprache und Altertumskunde* 42 (1905): 12–42.
33. Book of the Heavenly Cow; see Lichtheim, *Ancient Egyptian Literature*, vol. 2: *The New Kingdom* (Berkeley, 1976), pp. 197–199.
34. Book of Nut; cf. the translation of J. P. Allen, *Genesis in Egypt: The Philosophy of Ancient Egyptian Creation Accounts*, Yale Egyptological Studies 2, p. 1.
35. Book of the Heavenly Cow; see n. 33 above.
36. Prophecies of Neferti; cf. the translation of Lichtheim, *Ancient Egyptian Literature*, vol. 1: *The Old and Middle Kingdoms* (Berkeley, 1973), pp. 142–143.
37. Papyrus Leiden I 350, IV.16; cf. the translation of Wilson, *Ancient Near Eastern Texts*, p. 368.
38. Cf. the translation of A. Erman, *The Ancient Egyptians: A Sourcebook of Their Writings*, trans. A. M. Blackman (London, 1927; reprint ed. New York, 1966), p. 171.
39. Naos of Ismailiya, rear wall, line 5; see F. Ll. Griffith, *The Antiquities of Tell el Yahûdîyeh*, Egypt Exploration Society Memoir 7 (London, 1890), pl. 25, line 5; G. Goyon, *Kêmi* 6 (1936), pp. 14 (line 7), and 31.
40. Temple of Opet at Karnak; cf. the translation of C. de Wit, *Les Inscriptions du temple d'Opet, à Karnak*, vol. 3, Bibliotheca Aegyptiaca 13 (Brussels, 1968), p. 59.
41. Papyrus Berlin 3049, XV.9.
42. Instruction for Merikare; cf. the translation of Lichtheim, *Ancient Egyptian Literature*, vol. 1, p. 101.
43. Papyrus Berlin 3049, XII.
44. Temple of Opet; cf. the translation of de Wit, *Les Inscriptions du temple d'Opet*, p. 59.
45. Metternich Stela; see C. E. Sander-Hansen, *Die Texte der Metternichstele*, Analecta Aegyptiaca 7 (Copenhagen, 1956), pp. 64 and 68.
46. Great Hymn to the Aten; see Lichtheim, *Ancient Egyptian Literature*, vol. 2, p. 98.
47. S. Sauneron, *Le Temple d'Esna*, p. 17, lines 20–22.
48. See S. Sauneron, "La Différentiation des languages d'après la tradition égyptienne," *Bulletin de l'Institut Français d'Archéologie Orientale au Caire* 60 (1960): 31–40; J. Černý, "Thot as Creator of Languages," *Journal of Egyptian Archaeology* 34 (1948): 121–122.
49. R. A. Parker et al., *The Edifice of Taharqa by the Sacred Lake of Karnak*, Brown Egyptological Studies 8 (Providence, 1979), pl. 21.
50. Ibid., pl. 31. See also J. Assmann, *Der König als Sonnenpriester: Ein kosmographischer Begleittext zur kultischen Sonnenhymnik in thebanischen Tempeln und Gräbern*, Abhandlungen des Deutschen Archäologischen Instituts Kairo, Agyptologische Reihe 7 (Glückstadt, 1970), p. 21.
51. H. Te Velde, "Some Remarks on the Mysterious Language of the Baboons," in J. H. Kamstra, H. Milde, and K. Wagtendonk (eds.), *Funerary Symbols and*

Religion: Essays Dedicated to Professor M. S. H. G. Heerma van Voss (Kampen, 1988), pp. 129–137.
52. Stela of Ramesses II at Gebel el-Silsila; see K. A. Kitchen, *Ramesside Inscriptions: Historical and Biographical*, vol. 1 (Oxford, 1975), p. 86, line 5; P. Barguet, "Les Stèles du Nil," *Bulletin de l'Institut Français d'Archéologie Orientale au Caire* 50 (1952): 52 and 59; A. Barucq and F. Daumas, *Hymnes et prières de l'Égypte ancienne* (Paris, 1980), p. 503.
53. Papyrus Harris I, 75, 6; see P. Grandet, *Le Papyrus Harris I* (Cairo, 1994), vol. 1, p. 335 and vol. 2, p. 225. See also the Hymn to the Nile, Papyrus Sallier 2, XII, line 1; Lichtheim, *Ancient Egyptian Literature*, vol. 1, pp. 204–210.
54. Instruction of Any; cf. the translation of Lichtheim, *Ancient Egyptian Literature*, vol. 2, p. 141.
55. J. Assmann, *Ma'at: Gerechtigkeit und Unsterblichkeit im alten Ägypten* (Munich, 1990), pp. 192–195.

4
The Appearance of the Gods

1. Louvre C 286; Dynasty 18.
2. Book of the Dead, chaps. 76–78. See E. von Dassow (ed.), *The Egyptian Book of the Dead: The Book of Going Forth by Day* (San Francisco, 1994), pls. 25–26 and p. 108.
3. E. Hornung, *Conceptions of God in Ancient Egypt: The One and the Many*, trans. by John Baines (Ithaca, N.Y., 1982), pp. 127–128.
4. Papyrus Boulaq 17. See J. A. Wilson, in J. B. Pritchard (ed.), *Ancient Near Eastern Texts Relating to the Old Testament*, 2d ed. (Princeton, 1955), p. 366.
5. Papyrus British Museum 10042 (Magical Papyrus Harris 501), IV, line 9. See O. Lange, *Der Magische Papyrus Harris*, Kgl. Danske Videnskabernes Selskab, Historisk-Filologiske Meddelelser 14/2 (Copenhagen, 1927), pp. 38 and 41; J. Assmann, *Aegyptische Hymnen und Gebete* (Zurich, 1975), p. 295. See also the Myth of the Heavenly Cow, in which Re's bones are of silver and his flesh of gold; E. Hornung, *Der Ägyptische Mythos Von der Himmelskuh*, Orbis Biblicus et Orientalis 46 (Freiburg and Göttingen, 1982), pp. 1 and 37. Further, see the story of the birth of the royal children in Papyrus Westcar IX, lines 10, 18, and 25; M. Lichtheim, *Ancient Egyptian Literature*, vol. 1 (Berkeley, 1973), pp. 220–221 and G. Lefebvre, *Romans et Contes Égyptiens* (Paris, 1949), pp. 86–87.
6. Papyrus Berlin 13603. See W. Erichsen and S. Schott, *Fragmente Memphitischer Theologie* (1954), p. 65.
7. D. Meeks, in C. Malamoud and J.-P. Vernant (eds.), *Le Corps des dieux*, Le Temps de Réflection 7 (Paris, 1986), p. 184.

8. D. Meeks, *Revue de l'Histoire des Religions* 205 (1988): 433–434.
9. B. Williams, *Journal of the American Research Center in Egypt* 25 (1988): 35–59.

5
Divine Society

1. Papyrus Deir el-Medina 27. See S. Allam, *Hieratische ostraka und papyri aus der Ramessidenzeit* (Tübingen, 1973); D. Valbelle, *"Les Ouvriers de la Tombe": Deir el-Médineh à l'époque ramesside,* Bibliothèque d'Étude 96 (Cairo, 1985), pp. 236–238.
2. C. Leitz, *Tagenwählerei* (Wiesbaden, 1994), pl. 9; J. F. Borghouts, *Revue d'Égyptologie* 33 (1981): 19–20. For Leitz, the "thing" (determined by a phallus) done by Hedjhotep to Montu would be a simple allusion to Osirian rites. See B. Backes, *Enquête sur le dieu Hedjhotep,* Ph.D. diss., Institut d'Égyptologie de Strasbourg.
3. F. Lexa, *Papyrus Insinger: Les Enseignements moraux d'un scribe égyptien du premier siècle après J.-C., texte démotique avec transcription, traduction française, commentaire, vocabulaire et introduction grammaticale et littéraire* (Paris, 1926), vol. 2, p. 47, instr. 9. See M. Lichtheim, *Ancient Egyptian Literature,* vol. 3 (Berkeley, 1980), p. 192.
4. Coffin Texts, spell 334. See R. O. Faulkner, *The Ancient Egyptian Coffin Texts,* vol. 1 (Warminster, 1973), pp. 257–260.
5. H. Frankfort, *The Cenotaph of Seti I at Abydos* (London, 1933), vol. 1, pp. 83–86 and vol. 2, pl. 83; see also O. Neugebauer and R. A. Parker, *Egyptian Astronomical Texts,* vol. 1, pp. 67–81 and pls. 51–54.
6. G. T. Martin, *The Tomb-Chapel of Paser and Ra'ia at Saqqâra,* Egypt Exploration Society Memoir 52 (London, 1985), p. 5 and pl. 10 (3).
7. A. H. Gardiner, *The Royal Canon of Turin* (Oxford, 1959), pl. 1.

6
Divine Functions

1. For translation and discussion of texts accompanying the representation in Figure 6, see James P. Allen, *Genesis in Egypt: The Philosophy of Ancient Egyptian Creation Accounts,* Yale Egyptological Studies 2 (New Haven, Conn., 1988), pp. 1–7.
2. For this image of a bubble, see ibid., p. 7.
3. Stela from Gebel el-Silsila, see P. Barguet, *Bulletin de l'Institut Français d'Archéologie Orientale au Caire* 50 (1952): 52 and 59; A. Barucq and F. Daumas, *Hymnes et prières de l'Égypte ancienne* (Paris, 1980), p. 503.

4. On the Book of the Earth, see E. Hornung, *The Ancient Egyptian Books of the Afterlife*, trans. D. Lorton (Ithaca, N.Y., 1999), pp. 95–103.
5. G. Daressy, "Une Inondation à Thèbes sous le règne d'Osorkon II," *Receuil de Travaux Relatifs à la Philologie et à l'Archéologie Égyptiennes et Assyriennes* 18 (1896): 181, line 3.
6. Book of the Dead, chap. 175. For a translation, see C. Andrews (ed.), *The Egyptian Book of the Dead: The Book of Going Forth by Day* (San Francisco, 1994), pl. 29.
7. On this role of Hathor, see P. Derchain, *Hathor Quadrifrons: Recherches sur la Syntaxe d'un Mythe Égyptien*, Uitgaven van het Nederlands Historisch-Archaeologisch Instituut te Istanbul 28 (Istanbul, 1972).
8. P. Dem. Dodgson (Oxford 1932–1159). See F. de Cénival, *Revue d'Égyptologie* 32 (1983): 3–11.
9. Pyramid Texts, spell 600. For translation and discussion, see Allen, *Genesis in Egypt*, pp. 13–14.
10. Pyramid Texts, spell 527. See Allen, *Genesis in Egypt*, pp. 13–14.
11. For translation and discussion of the material, see ibid., pp. 14–27.
12. Papyrus Bremner-Rhind XXVI, line 22. See Allen, *Genesis in Egypt*, p. 28.
13. Coffin Texts, spell 647. For translation and discussion, see Allen, *Genesis in Egypt*, pp. 39–41.
14. For translation and discussion of the text, see ibid., pp. 42–47.
15. S. Sauneron, *Les fêtes Religieuses d'Esna aux derniers siècles du paganisme*, Esna 5 (Cairo, 1962), p. 89 (Esna 249, 2); see also pp. 88 (Esna 318, 11), 366 (Esna 261, 18), and 396 (Esna 262, 22).
16. E. Chassinat, *Le Temple d'Edfou*, vol. 6, Mémoires Publiés par les Membres de la Mission Archéologique Française au Caire 23 (Cairo, 1931), p. 247. See M.-L. Ryhiner, *L'Offrande du lotus dan les temples égyptiens d'Époque Tardive* (Brussels, 1986), p. 54.
17. Chassinat, *Temple d'Edfou*, vol. 6, pp. 14–15. See J. C. Goyon, *Les Dieux-gardiens et la genèse des temples* (Cairo, 1985), vol. 1, pp. 30–32.
18. For a translation of the text, see M. Lichtheim, *Ancient Egyptian Literature: A Book of Readings*, vol. 1: *The Old and Middle Kingdoms* (Berkeley, Calif., 1973), pp. 97–109.
19. Book of the Dead, chap. 175; see Andrews (ed.), *The Egyptian Book of the Dead*, pl. 29.
20. For the text, see H. W. Fairman, *The Triumph of Horus: An Ancient Egyptian Sacred Drama* (London, 1974).
21. See the study by K. Sethe, *Amun und die acht Urgötter von Hermopolis: eine Untersuchung über Ursprung und Wesen des ägyptischen Götterkönigs*, Abhandlungen der Deutschen Akademie der Wissenschaften zu Berlin,

Philosophisch-Historische Klasse, Jahrgang 1929, Nr. 4 (Berlin, 1929). For more recent research on this theology, see M. Doresse, *Revue d'Égyptologie* 23 (1971): 113–136 and *Revue d'Égyptologie* 25 (1973): 154–160; C. Traunecker, *La Chapelle d'Achoris à Karnak*, vol. 2 (Paris, 1981).

22. C. Traunecker, "Le Papyrus Spiegelberg et l'évolution des liturgies thébaines," in S. P. Vleeming (ed.), *Hundred-Gated Thebes: Acts of a Colloquium on Thebes and the Theban Area in the Graeco-Roman Period* (Leiden, 1995), pp. 183–201. On these cults and their relationship to the theoretical royalty of the Ptolemaic kings (cult of the crowns), see C. Traunecker, "Une Famille de prêtres à Karnak aux 1er et 2e siècles Avant J.-C.: Les Horsaisis-Nekhtmontou," in *Egyptian Religion: Studies Dedicated to the Memory of Jan Quaegebeur* (Leuven, 1998), pp. 1191–1230.
23. C. Traunecker, "Un Exemple de rite de substitution: Une Stèle de Nectanébo Ier," *Karnak* 7 (1983): 339–354.
24. C. Traunecker and F. Laroche, "La Chapelle adossée au temple de Khonsou," *Karnak* 6 (1980): 179–196.
25. J. Quaegebeur, "Les Saints égyptiens préchrétiens," *Orientalia Lovaniensia Periodica* 8 (1977): 129–143; idem, *Coptos: Hommes et dieux sur le parvis de Geb* (Louvain, 1992), pp. 387–391; G. Wagner, *Zeitschrift für Papyrologie und Epigraphik* 111 (1996): 97–113.
26. E. Chassinat and F. Daumas, *Le Temple de Dendara*, vol. 6 (Cairo, 1965), p. 91, line 8.
27. L. Pantalacci, "*Wnm-Hw33t*: Genèse et carrière d'un génie funéraire," *Bulletin de l'Institut Français d'Archéologie Orientale au Caire* 83 (1983): 297–312.
28. See A. Piankoff, *The Litany of Re*, Bollingen Series 40/4 (New York, 1964); E. Hornung, *The Ancient Egyptian Books of the Afterlife*, trans. D. Lorton (Ithaca, N.Y., 1999), pp. 136–147.
29. For translation and discussion, see Allen, *Genesis in Egypt*, pp. 52–54.
30. See J. Assmann, *The Search for God in Ancient Egypt*, trans. D. Lorton (Ithaca, 2001), pp. 235–243.
31. Allen, *Genesis in Egypt*, p. 53.
32. Great Hymn to the Aten; for a translation, see M. Lichtheim, *Ancient Egyptian Literature: A Book of Readings*, vol. 2: *The New Kingdom*, pp. 96–100.
33. C. Traunecker, "Aménophis IV et Nefertiti," *Bulletin de la Société Française d'Égyptologie* 107 (1986): 17–44. Idem, "Nefertiti, la Reine sans nom," *Égypte, Afrique et Orient* 14 (Aug.–Oct. 1999): 3–14.
34. C. Traunecker, "Données nouvelles sur le début du règne d'Aménophis IV et son oeuvre à Karnak," communication presented at the Third International Congress of Egyptology, Toronto, 1982; see *Journal of the Society for the Study of Egyptian Antiquities* 14/3 (1983): 60–70.

35. E. Hornung, *Akhenaten and the Religion of Light*, trans. D. Lorton (Ithaca, N.Y., 1999), pp. 54–55.

7
The Gods and the Human Realm

1. P. Derchain, *Revue d'Égyptologie* 27 (1975): 110–116 and *Revue d'Égyptologie* 30 (1978): 57.
2. See J. H. Breasted, *Ancient Records of Egypt* (New York, 1906), vol. 2, pp. 320–324; B. M. Bryan, *The Reign of Thutmose IV* (Baltimore, Md., 1991), pp. 145–146.
3. Stela Naples 1035. See O. Perdu, "Le Monument de Samtoutefnakht à Naple," *Revue d'Égyptologie* 36 (1985): 99–109.
4. A. Erman, *The Ancient Egyptians: A Sourcebook of Their Writings*, trans. A. M. Blackman (London, 1927; reprinted, New York, 1966), pp. 35–36.
5. S. Sauneron, *Le Papyrus magique illustré de Brooklyn (Brooklyn Museum) 47.218.156* (New York, 1970), p. 24.
6. Papyrus Leiden I 350, IV, line 25. See A. H. Gardiner, *Zeitschrift für Ägyptische Sprache und Altertumskunde* 42 (1906): 35; A. Barucq and F. Daumas, *Hymnes et Prières de l'Égypte Ancienne* (Paris, 1980), p. 225.
7. E. von Dassow (ed.), *The Egyptian Book of the Dead: The Book of Going Forth by Day* (San Francisco, 1994), p. 103.
8. Breasted, *Ancient Records of Egypt*, vol. 1, pp. 211–212.
9. Ibid., vol. 2, pp. 55–68.
10. For example, the Contendings of Horus and Seth; see M. Lichtheim, *Ancient Egyptian Literature: A Book of Readings*, vol. 2: *The New Kingdom* (Berkeley, Calif., 1976), pp. 214–223.
11. See J. Quaegebeur, J.-M. Kruchten, and C. Traunecker in *Oracles et prophéties dans l'antiquité: Colloque de Strasbourg 15–17 juin 1995* (Paris, 1997).
12. Breasted, *Ancient Records of Egypt*, vol. 2, pp. 326–329; Bryan, *The Reign of Thutmose IV*, pp. 333–334.
13. Breasted, *Ancient Records of Egypt*, vol. 2, p. 116.
14. Maat as the principle of social cohesion is the central theme of J. Assmann's study, *Maat: L'Égypte pharaonique et l idée de justice sociale* (Paris, 1984).
15. The "Pharaoh ludens" concept was introduced by E. Hornung, *Eranos* 512 (1982): 479–518.
16. J. F. Borghouts, "Divine Interventions in Ancient Egypt," in R. J. Demarée and J. J. Janssen (eds.), *Gleanings from Deir el-Medîna* (Leiden, 1982); see also J. G. Griffiths in *Pyramid Studies and Other Essays Presented to I. E. S. Edwards* (London, 1988), pp. 92–102.

17. P. Vernus, "Le Dieu personnel dans l'Égypte pharaonique," in *Colloques d'histoire des religions organisés par la Société Ernest Renant, Société Française d'Histoire des Religions* (1977), pp. 143–157.
18. Traunecker, "L'Appel au divin: La Crainte des dieux et les serments de temple," in *Oracles et Prophéties dans l'Antiquité*.

8
Geography and the Gods

1. Papyrus Insinger 28.4; see M. Lichtheim, *Ancient Egyptian Literature: A Book of Readings*, vol. 3, *The Late Period* (Berkeley, 1980), pp. 184–217.
2. E. Chassinat and F. Daumas, *Le Temple de Dendara*, vol. 8 (Cairo, 1978), p. 131, lines 13–14. See F. Daumas, "Quelques textes de l'atelier des orfèvres dans le temple de Dendara," in *Livre du Centenaire: 1880–1980*, p. 115; and P. Derchain, "L'Atelier des orfèvres à Dendara et les origines de l'alchimie," *Chronique d'Égypte* 65 (1990): 236.
3. See Lichtheim, *Ancient Egyptian Literature*, vol. 2, *The New Kingdom* (Berkeley, Calif., 1976), pp. 135–146.
4. Speos Artemidos inscription; see J. H. Breasted, *Ancient Records of Egypt* (New York, 1906; reprinted, New York, 1962), vol. 2, pp. 122–126.
5. Papyrus Turin 1974 + 1945. See J. Černý, *Late Ramesside Letters*, Bibliotheca Aegyptiaca 9 (Brussels, 1939), p. 39, lines 7–8; E. Wente, *Late Ramesside Letters*, p. 55.
6. H. Junker, *Der grosse Pylon des Tempels der Isis in Philä* (Vienna, 1958), p. 90, lines 18–19.
7. C. Traunecker, "La Revanche du crocodile de Coptos," in *Mélanges Adolphe Gutbub* (Montpellier, 1984), pp. 219–229.
8. P. Derchain, "L'Auteur du papyrus Jumilhac," *Revue d'Égyptologie* 41 (1990): 9–30.
9. See J. A. Wilson, in J. B. Pritchard (ed.), *Ancient Near Eastern Texts Relating to the Old Testament*, 2d ed. (Princeton, 1955), pp. 199–201.
10. See ibid., pp. 17–18.
11. Here, we must note the astonishing head, now in Strasbourg, which represents a Persian king or god in Egyptian style. It could be a representation of Atum/Ahura-Mazda; see C. Traunecker, "Un Portrait ignoré d'un roi perse: La Tête 'Strasbourg 1604,'" *Transeuphratène* 9 (1995): 101–117.
12. Breasted, *Ancient Records of Egypt*, vol. 4, pp. 87–206; for the passage in question, see p. 123.
13. Bentresh Stela; see Lichtheim, *Ancient Egyptian Literature*, vol. 3, pp. 90–94.

Bibliography

Allen, J. P. *Genesis in Egypt: The Philosophy of Ancient Egyptian Creation Accounts.* Yale Egyptological Studies 2. New Haven, Conn., 1988.
Assmann, J. *The Search for God in Ancient Egypt.* Ithaca, N.Y., 2001.
———. *Mâat: L'Égypte pharaonique et l'idée de justice sociale.* Paris, 1989.
Bonhême, M. A., and A. Forgeau. *Pharaon: Les Secrets du pouvoir.* Paris, 1988.
Derchain, P. "Anthropologie." In *Dictionnaire des mythologies*, edited by Yves Bonnefoy. Paris, 1981.
———. "Cosmogonie." In *Dictionnaire des mythologies*, edited by Yves Bonnefoy. Paris, 1981.
———. "Divinité." In *Dictionnaire des mythologies*, edited by Yves Bonnefoy. Paris, 1981.
———. "Rituels." In *Dictionnaire des mythologies*, edited by Yves Bonnefoy. Paris, 1981.
———. "La Religion égyptienne." In vol. 2 of *Histoire des religions*, edited by H.-C. Puech, pp. 63–140. Encyclopédie de la Pléiade 34. Paris, 1970.
———. *Le Papyrus Salt 825 (BM 10051): Rituel pour la conservation de la vie en Égypte.* 2 vols. Koninklijke Academie van België, Verhandelingen 58. Brussels, 1965.
Dunand, F., and C. Zivie-Coche. *Dieux et hommes en Égypte.* Paris, 1991.
Hornung, E. *Conceptions of God in Ancient Egypt: The One and the Many.* Ithaca, N.Y., 1982.
Kees, H. *Der Götterglaube im alten Ägypten.* Leipzig, 1941.
Lessing, E., and P. Vernus. *Dieux de l'Égypte.* Paris, 1998.
Lévêque, J. *Sagesses de l'Égypte ancienne.* Supplément au Cahier Évangile 46. Paris, 1983.

Meeks, D. "Notion de 'dieu' et structure du panthéon dans l'Égypte ancienne." *Revue d'Histoire des Religions* 204 (1988): 425–446.

———. "Zoomorphie et image des dieux dans l'Égypte ancienne." In *Corps des dieux. Le Temps de réflexion 7*, pp. 171–191. Paris, 1986.

———. "Génies, anges et démons en Égypte." In *Génies, anges et démons: Egypte, Babylone, Israël, Islam, peuples altaïques, Inde, Birmanie, Asie du Sud-Est, Tibet, Chine*. Sources Orientales 8. Paris, 1971.

Morenz, S. *Egyptian Religion*. Ithaca, N.Y., 1973.

Quirke, S. *Ancient Egyptian Religion*. London, 1992.

Sauneron, S. *The Priests of Ancient Egypt*. Ithaca, N.Y., 2000.

Sauneron, S., and J. Yoyotte. "La Naissance du monde selon l'Égypte ancienne." In *La Naissance du monde: Égypte ancienne, Sumer, Akkad, Hourrites et Hittites, Canaan, Israel, Islam, Turcs et Mongols, Iran préislamique, Inde, Siam, Laos, Tibet, Chine*. Sources Orientales 1. Paris, 1958.

Shafer, B., ed. *Religion in Ancient Egypt: Gods, Myths, and Personal Practice*. Ithaca, N.Y., 1991.

Traunecker, C. "De l'hiérophanie au temple." In *Religion und Philosophie im alten Ägypten: Festgabe für Philippe Derchain zu seinem 65. Geburtstag am, 24 juli 1991. Orientalia Lovaniensia Analecta 39*, edited by U. Verhoeven and E. Graefe, pp. 303–317. Leuven, 1991.

———. "Observations sur le décor des temples égyptiens." In, *L'Image et la production du sacré: Actes du colloque de Strasbourg, 20–21 janvier 1988*, edited by F. Dunand, J.-M. Spieser, and J. Wirth, pp. 77–101. Paris, 1991.

Reference Works

Baines, J., and J. Malek. *Cultural Atlas of Ancient Egypt*. New York, 2000.

Bonnet, H. *Reallexikon der ägyptischen Religion*. Berlin, 1952.

Helck, W., and E. Otto. *Lexikon der Ägyptologie*. 7 vols. Wiesbaden, 1972–1991.

Posener, G., S. Sauneron, and J. Yoyotte. *Dictionnaire de la civilisation égyptienne*. Paris, 1959.

Translations of Texts

Barguet, P. *Textes des sarcophages égyptiens du Moyen Empire*. Paris, 1986.

———. *Le Livre des morts des anciens Égyptiens*. Paris, 1967.

Barucq, A. and F. Daumas. *Hymnes et prières de l'Égypte ancienne*. Paris, 1980.

Goyon, J.-C. *Rituels funéraires de l'ancienne Égypte*. Paris, 1972.

Index

Action, in ritual, 13
Akh
  divine personality and, 34
  significance of notion of, 23–24
Akhenaten, 90, 91. *See also* Amenophis IV
Akhsu, function of, 67
Amélineau, Émile, 9
  and older theories of gods, 25
Amenhotpe, accession to divinity by, 64
Amenophis II, 106
Amenophis IV, Atenism and, 90–91
Amun
  *ba*s of, 88, 89f
  as creator god, 74
  divine sovereignty of, 66
  family triad of, 60
  immanence and transcendence of, 88–89
  in Nubia, 105
  and ritual of mammisi, 59
  secret name of, 32
Amun of Opet, 83
Amun-Re, as supreme being, 9
Anat, role of, 107
Androgyny, and sexuality of deities, 45–46
Animals, and communication with the divine, 96
Ankh, as divine accessory, 50

Anthropomorphization, of deities, 29, 43–44
Antywy, 60
Anukis, 60
Apis, animal form of, 48, 49f, 96
Apopis, 85–86
  stopping of time by, 39
Arnobius, on Egyptian theology, 8
Assmann, Jan, 11
Astarte, role of, 107
At, divine time and, 38
Aten
  Amenophis IV and, 90–91
  in cosmology of the sun, 76
  hymns to, 4
Atum, in cosmology of the sun, 76

Ba
  divine personality and, 33
  significance of notion of, 22–23
Ba-birds, 47–48
Baboons, divine language of, 40
Bakennifi the Athribite, accession to divinity by, 64
Bau
  divine personality and, 33
  writings as, 23
Benu, role of in creation myth, 77
Bes, 93–94

129

Index

Births, divine, 58–59
Bisexuality, of deities, 45
Body, role of, 20
Book of Going Forth by Day, 2. *See also* Book of the Dead
Book of the Dead, 2, 94
Book of the Faiyum, 6, 103
Book of the Heavenly Cow, 5, 12f
    divine time and, 37
Book of the Sky, 63
Books of Breathing, 4

Children, gods as, 59
City gods, 99–101. *See also* Deities; Gods
Clement of Alexandria, on Egyptian theology, 8
Coffin Texts, 2
    creation stories in, 70
    creator god in, 76
    immaterial space in, 78
Combat, punitive vs. primordial in creation myths, 82
Communication, means of, 92–95
    from divine realm to humans, 92–94
    from humans to the divine, 94–95
Cosmogony
    of Edfu, 81–82
    Heliopolitan, 74–76, 75f
    Hermopolitan, 73
    procedures of, 76–80
        creator and will to create in, 76–77
        images of, 79–80
        immaterial space in, 78
        primeval mound in, 77
        word and thought in, 78–79
    Theban, 77
Cosmology, creation and, 71–72, 72f
Created World, humans in, 19
Creation, 70–76
    cosmological imagery of, 71–72, 72f
    deities and concepts of, 74–76
    inorganic model of, 80
    precreation and, 72–74
    process of, 78–79
    stories of, 70–71
Creator god, 74, 76–77, 83–84. *See also* Creation; Deities; Gods
Crocodile, ambivalence of form of, 16

Cults
    daily rituals of, 4
    of kings, 65

Daily Cult Ritual, 4
Dedwen, 105
Deification, of kings, 65
Deities. *See also* Gods; *specific deities*
    archaeological evidence of, 26
    bodies of, 43–48
        age of, 44–45
        androgyny of, 45–46
        animal forms of, 48, 50f
        anthropomorphism and, 43–44
        hybrid forms of, 46–48
        materials of, 44
    clothing of, 54–55
    crowds of, 62, 63f
    crowns and headgear of, 55
    divine accessories of, 50–53
        hieroglyphs for, 52f
    exported, 108–110
    family models of, 57–60
        child gods in, 59
        couples and consorts in, 57–58
        families and triads in, 60
        procreation and rebirth in, 58–59
    foreign, 106–108
    groups of, 60–62
    hierarchy and recruitment of, 62–69
        accession to divinity, 62–64
        divine sovereignties, 65–66
        genies and demons, 66–69
    images to be read by, 56
    and individuals, 97–98
    and kings, 96–97
    lists of, 6, 7f
    of marches and frontiers, 103–106
    natural settings and, 16
    Nubian, 105–106
    as personifications of cities, 100–101
    physical appearance of, 42–43
    postures of, 48–50
    of provinces, 101–103
        geographic lists of, 102
    sources concerning, 1–3
    special functions of, 86–91
Demons, function of, 67–69

Index

Derchain, Philippe, 10
Description de l'Égypte, concepts of Egyptian theology in, 9
Desert, deities of, 103–104
Diodorus Siculus, on Egyptian theology, 8
Divine, the. *See also* Deities; Gods
  accession to by private individuals, 62–63
  language of, 39–40
  nature of, 29–35
    elements of personality of, 33–35
    names of, 30–33
    terminology of, 29–30, 30f
    space and, 35–37
    subsistence of, 40–41
    time and, 37–39
Djeme, dead gods of, 84
Djeser, terminology of the divine and, 30
Djet
  divine time and, 37–38
  role of, 20
Duat, divine time and, 36–37
Dyads, of deities, 60–61
Dynasty 1, 28
Dynasty 3, theologies of, 29
Dynasty 21, divine sovereignty of, 66

Earthquakes, symbolism of, 18
Edfu, cosmogony of, 81–82
Enlightenment, concepts of Egyptian theology during, 8–9
Ennead of Heliopolis, 61
Enneads, of deities, 61–62
Epithets, 31. *See also* Names
Erman, Adolf, 10
Esna, cosmogony of, 82
Eudoxus of Cnidus, on Egyptian theology, 7

Frankfort, Henri, 10, 26

Geb
  divine sovereignty of, 65–66
  in Heliopolitan Cosmogony, 74
Gender, of deities, 45–46
Genies, function of, 66, 67
Geographical Papyrus of Brooklyn, 6
Gods. *See also* Deities; Divine, the
  dead, 84
  healing, 93

older theories of, 25–26
Primeval, 83–84
Great Sphinx at Giza, 107
Greco-Roman Period, mythological creation stories in, 71
Greece
  concepts of Egyptian theology in, 7–8
  and divine language in Egypt, 40

Hapy
  androgyny of, 45–46
  function of, 67
Haremhab of Naukratis, accession to divinity by, 64
Harpokrates, as a child, 59
Hathor, 16
  in Nubia, 105
Hathor columns, hybrid forms of deities and, 46–47
Hau, role of, 20
Haurun, and Great Sphinx at Giza, 107
Heart
  divine personality and, 34
  role of, 20–21
Heb, function of, 67
Hedjhotep, function of, 67
Hehu, precreation and, 73
Heliopolitan Cosmogony, 74–76, 75f
Hermopolitan tradition, cosmogony of, 73
Hornung, Erik, 11
Horus
  of Edfu, 51f
  hybrid form of, 47f
  myth of, 81–82
  in Nubia, 105
  and Seth, 61
Hu, and Sia, 61
Humankind, role of, 19–24
  in the Created World, 19
  in the Imaginary, 21–24
  in the Real, 20–21, 20f
Hymns, 4–5
  to the Aten, 4
Hymn to the Nile, 4
Ib, role of, 20–21
Ibu, accession to divinity by, 64
Ihy, 59
  conception of, 58

Illness, demons and, 68
Imaginary, the, humans in, 21–22
Imenhy, function of, 67
Imhotep, accession to divinity by, 64
Instruction for Merikare, creation myth in, 80–81
Iru, 42–43
Isis
　in Heliopolitan Cosmogony, 75
　and Nephthys, 61
　and secret name of Re, 31–33
Iusaas, role of in creation myth, 77
Izi, accession to divinity by, 64

Jêquier, Gustave, and older theories of gods, 25

Ka
　divine personality and, 33–34
　significance of notion of, 21–22
Kagemni, accession to divinity by, 64
Kees, Hermann, 10
　and older theories of gods, 25–26
Keku, precreation and, 73
Khat, role of, 20
Kheperu, 42–43
Khepri, in cosmology of the sun, 76
Khnum, 60
Khons, family triad of, 60
Kingship, 18
　deification and, 65
　deities and, 96–97
　evolution of concept of, 28
　and ritual of mammisi, 59
Kircher, Athanasius, on Egyptian theology, 8
Kom Ombo, temple at, 23–24, 24f

Landscape, symbolic importance of, 15
Language, divine, 39–40
Lion, ambivalence of form of, 16. *See also* Sakhmet
Loret, Victor, 9
　and older theories of gods, 25
Lotus, role of in creation myths, 79

Maat
　concept of, 96–97
　role of in creation myth, 81
Maaty, 60–61
Magical texts, creation stories in, 71
Mammisi, ritual of, 58–59
Masturbation, role of in creation myths, 76–77
Menket, function of, 67
Mer, function of, 67
Merekhet, function of, 67
Meret-goddesses, 62
Middle Kingdom, cosmogony of, 73
Min, postures of, 49–50
Modern School, of Egyptian religion, 10–11
Monotheism, 9–10
Montu, 57
　patronage of, 98
Morenz, Siegfried, 26
Moret, Alexandre, 9
　and older theories of gods, 25
Mut, family triad of, 60
Myths, as historical source, 5

Names
　divine, 30–33
　programmatic, 31
　role of, 21
　secret, 31–33
Naqada II Period, 28f
　conceptions of afterlife during, 26
　theologies of, 27–29
Naqada III Period, theologies of, 27–29
Nature
　order of, 16, 17–19
　role of, 10
Nebethetepet, role of in creation myth, 77
Neferhotep, 59
　accession to divinity by, 64
Nefertem, 60
　function of, 67
Neheh, divine time and, 37–38
Neith, androgyny of, 45
Nekhbet, 68
　and Wadjit, 61
Neper, function of, 67

Nephthys
  in Heliopolitan Cosmogony, 75
  and Isis, 61
Nespamedu of Elephantine, accession to divinity by, 64
Netjer, terminology of the divine and, 29–30
Nile, importance of, 14–16, 18
Nomes, deities of, 101–102
Nubia, deities of, 105–106
Numbers, divine, 61–62
Nun, precreation and, 73–74
Nut
  children of, 58–59
  in Heliopolitan Cosmogony, 74
  role of in creation, 72

Ogdoad, Hermopolitan, 61
Old Kingdom, polytheism of, 9
Opening of the Mouth Ritual, 4
  communication and, 95
Oracles, communication with the divine via, 94–95
Order, political, natural order and, 18–19
Osiris
  divine accessories of, 52
  divine sovereignty of, 65–66
  in Heliopolitan Cosmogony, 75
  myths of, 86–87, 88

Papyrus Brooklyn 47.218.84, 103
Papyrus Jumilhac, 6, 103
Pehu, function of, 67
Pepinakht, accession to divinity by, 64
Personality, divine, elements of, 33–35
  akh, 34
  ba and *bas*, 33
  heart, 34
  ka and *kas*, 33–34
  sekhem, 34–35
  shadow, 34
Physics, religion as, 11–12
Plato, on Egyptian theology, 8
Plutarch, myth of Osiris of, 87
Polysemy, in ritual, 13
Polytheism, 9–10
Popular piety, 95
Power, political, and access to deities, 29

Primeval Mound, role of in creation myth, 77
Profane sources, of history of deities, 1–2
Provinces, deities and, 101–103
Ptah
  divine sovereignty of, 66
  patronage of, 98
Pyramid Texts, 2, 3f
  akh in, 24
  polytheism of, 9
  precreation in, 73
  Tefnut in, 75
Pythagoras, on Egyptian theology, 7

Qadesh, 108, 109f

Rainfall, symbolism of, 18
Ramesside Period, conception of Amun during, 88–89
Re
  and Apopis, 86
  bas of, 33
  secret name of, 31–33
  and Seth, 85
Real, the, humans in, 20–21, 20f
Reality, nature as, 11–12
Re-Horakhty, divine accessories of, 53f
Religious sources, of history of deities, 1, 2
Religious texts, major corpora, 2–4
Renaissance, concepts of Egyptian theology during, 8
Renenutet, function of, 67
Reshep, role of, 106–107
Ritual, 4
  dangerous nature of, 5–6
  importance of, 12–13
  performative nature of, 13
Royal Canon of Turin, divine sovereignty of, 66
Ruty of Leontopolis, 60

Sakhmet, 16, 17f, 68
  Litanies of, 69
  patronage of, 98
Satis, 60
Sauneron, Serge, 10
  on notion of *ba*, 23

Sekhem, divine personality and, 34–35
Sekhet, function of, 67
Sematawytefnakhte, 92–93
Serpent, ambivalence of form of, 16. *See also* Apopis
Seth, 85–86
 birth of, 58
 in Heliopolitan Cosmogony, 75
 and Horus, 61
Sethe, Kurt, 10
 on totemic theory of gods, 25
Shabaka Stone, creation myth of, 78–79, 80
Shadow
 divine personality and, 34
 role of, 20
Shesemu, function of, 67
Shu
 in Heliopolitan Cosmogony, 74
 as metaphor for immaterial space, 78
 role of in creation, 72
Shut, role of, 20
Sia, and Hu, 61
Sopd, 104–105
Sovereignties, divine, 65–66
Space
 divine, 35–37
  boundaries of, 35
  and distancing of the divine, 35–36
  Duat as, 36
  nearby spaces and, 36
 immaterial, 78
Speech
 performative nature of, 13
 in process of creation, 78–79
Spitting, role of in creation myth, 77
Sun
 birth of, 84
 cosmology of, 76
 divine sovereignty of, 65
 role of in creation, 72
Symbols, divine, 26

Tayt, function of, 67
Tefnut
 in Heliopolitan Cosmogony, 74
 role of in creation myth, 77
Temples
 economy and, 18
 libraries of, 5
Tenmet, function of, 67
Tenmu, precreation and, 73
Thales, on Egyptian theology, 7
That Which Is in the Duat, 3
Theology, Greek perceptions of Egyptian, 7–8
Thoth
 divine language and, 39
 hybrid forms of, 46, 47f
 in Nubia, 105
 patronage of, 98
Thought
 and action, in ritual, 12
 in process of creation, 78–79
Throne, as divine accessory, 52–53, 53f
Time, divine, 37–39
 end of, 38–39
 passage of, 38
 two eternities of, 37–38
Totemistic societies, polytheism and, 9–10
Triads, of deities, 60
Trigger, B. G., and contemporary theories of gods, 27
Truth, multiplicity of, 11

Universe, organization of, 80–86
 creator god and dead gods in, 83–84
 fomenters of trouble in, 85–86
 golden age and revolt in, 80–83

Victorious Thebes, 100–101
Virey, Philippe, 9
 and older theories of gods, 25

Wadjit, and Nekhbet, 61
Wadj-wer, function of, 67
Wakha, accession to divinity by, 64
Was-scepter, as divine accessory, 50–51
We, function of, 67
Wepwawet, animal form of, 48
Words, in process of creation, 78–79
Writing, as *bau*, 23

Yoyotte, Jean, 10